Niff –
Laugh at life!,
Diane Pascoe

Life Isn't Perfect, but My Lipstick Is

Real life. Real laughs.

DIANE PASCOE

ISBN: 1976575761
ISBN-13: 9781976575761
Library of Congress Control Number: 2017914757
CreateSpace Independent Publishing Platform
North Charleston, South Carolina

DEDICATION

To Mom: You always believed in my ability to do whatever I set my mind to do. You nurtured my creativity in any project I undertook. Thank you for bringing out the best in me. I love you.

CONTENTS

INTRODUCTION

When our family moved from the Land of the Mounties to the Land of Y'all in June 2004, I considered myself to be somewhat retired. My husband, Eric, whom I affectionately call Honey or Love God, considered my unemployment to be a temporary career pause—a long vacation, really. He regularly asked how my job search was going. Did I dare tell him that it was stuck in neutral, maybe even in reverse?

I had a dilemma: if I did start looking for work, I would be forced to finish my résumé. This was difficult because I always got stuck at the part where I had to write my employment objective, as I had none.

But there were other barriers to job hunting—nobody hired in the summer, and then it was only a few months to Christmas, when no one would be hiring either. It was looking as though my career pause would continue through the new year. This would be the perfect time to rethink my talents, my passions, and the things that bring me joy. Exploring my potential was the *real* adventure in our move to Raleigh—a journey into the unknown—and it was the journey that was so refreshing. The *corporate voices* I had heard for twenty-five years had been silenced at last, and I was able to hear *my own voice* much more clearly. I realized, through this process, that my dream was to write humor, so I used this time to write about the funny and fascinating everyday moments in my life.

Looking back, my passion for writing humor had been ignited in tenth grade English, when I easily wrote an essay on "My Most Embarrassing Moment." After the exams were graded, the teacher told the class she was going to read a very funny essay aloud, and after she had read the first few words, I realized she was reading *my* essay! This was the first time I knew that I could write stories which others found funny.

Since my career pause, I have written about such things as being fired as the kindergarten rhythm-band conductor, my lipstick obsession, my yo-yo weight, my snoring, and my gray hair, but also my dreams and triumphs, in a way that is hopefully relatable and human.

I have also written about my Love God and me, our two dogs, and our youngest son, Braden, who was twelve when we moved to North Carolina, despite his insisting that he wasn't moving. Our promise of a dog changed his thinking. Our three older children, who were grown and living in Canada, were spared my literary scalpel.

Of course, my Love God, always the opportunist, quickly developed a marketing plan for my life stories. "Maybe you can step up your scribing activities a bit and charge, say, ten cents for each story you e-mail out," he said encouragingly.

Oh sure. Let me see now...by my calculations, I should make about eighty cents a week, given that most readers will delete my ditties when they arrive in their e-mail inbox with an invoice. If you include my parents, sisters, and a few loyal friends, I might have sixteen paying readers, although I suspect that half these readers will demand a refund once they see my typos, non sequiturs, and dangling participles, because I write like I speak—where nothing follows and everything dangles. *Scrap the humor-by-e-mail idea, Honey.*

As I have grown older, I have freed myself to be a better me—a wiser, more confident, funnier version of my younger, safer, unexamined self. Fat or thin, gray hair or brown hair, funny or not—I have family and friends who bring me pleasure, pride, and peace.

Oh yes—I found a fabulous position in human resources in the new year, just as I had hoped, but I also continued writing about the ordinary and extraordinary events of my life in a way that I hope will bring a smile to readers' lips.

Life is so much better when you're laughing!

HOW HE PROPOSED
MARRIAGE...SORT OF

"Are we ever going to get married?"

My question hung heavily in the air on that snowy New Year's Day. I looked over at Honey to see if he was still breathing, and his strained face looked like he was about to pass through the pearly gates.

I'd been thinking a lot about marriage that holiday season, secretly hoping that he might surprise me for Christmas and spring for a ring. Instead, I got a cookbook and a Crock-Pot, neither of which I could wear on my finger. Call me crazy, but given we were in love and had been together for more than three years, I really felt it was time to make it official and tie the knot. As Honey often says when I'm waiting too long at a traffic light, "The light isn't going to get any greener, dear."

The question about marriage wasn't my first crack at the subject that week. Only the day before, I'd told Honey that I was thinking of going back to my maiden name, as I'd kept the last name of my ex-husband, Mr. Wrong, well past its expiration date, mainly for convenience. Changing my name required heaps of correspondence with three levels of government—plus an update to Santa Claus so that he knew who and where I was. I hoped it would dawn on Honey that it was time for me to change my last name to his, but alas—no proposal, no ring.

"But I think we're doing just fine without being married, don't you?" Honey countered.

Is there a man alive who doesn't think like this? Darn it, Dad was right. If Honey could get the milk over the fence, he wouldn't need to buy the cow. Too late to cry over spilled milk, fences, and cows. I was on a mission.

"No, we aren't doing fine at all," I declared. "I think it's time for us to get married."

"But I was waiting to buy you the perfect diamond ring!" he sputtered as I watched his nose grow right before my tearing eyes. He was smart enough to know it was time to wave the white flag. "OK, all right. So when do you want to get married?"

Yes! Strike while the iron is hot. I wiped away my perfectly timed tears. "How about six weeks from now, on Saturday, February sixteenth?"

"Yup, that'll work well for me—one gift each year on February fifteenth will cover both Valentine's Day on the fourteenth *and* our anniversary on the sixteenth."

I ignored his frugal thinking as I marked M-day on the calendar in large letters with a permanent, nonerasable marker. Mission accomplished. It was time to plan a wedding.

It was a second marriage for both of us, and with sketchy churchgoing habits, we wanted to find a mobile minister who'd marry us at home. I looked through the newspaper and found Reverend Diane from the Church of Unity, Lightness, and Lollipops—*or* something vaguely new age—whose office was conveniently nestled between a Dunkin' Donuts and a Subway at the shopping center. We had found ourselves a preacher on wheels.

The big day finally came. My wedding outfit was a sailor-style blouse and skirt that made it look as though our wedding night might be my last kick at romance before I shipped out to sea. My bangs were lacquered into a natty tidal-wave sculpture that floated just above my forehead, and I had plastered on full war paint, including lipstick that didn't smear or smudge but also didn't wash off. I'd spend our wedding night sleeping in nonremovable ruby-red lipstick.

We all assembled for the ceremony in the living room, except for my sister, who was missing the sacred ceremony in favor of a quick smoke. Reverend Diane led us solemnly through our vows until we were stopped by the sound of our kids giggling at our younger son, who was staring up at the ceiling like it was the Sistine Chapel. As if that weren't enough, the video camera picked that moment to run out of power. The shopping-center minister halted the ceremony until we all got back on track, and then we continued with our vows until at last we were married. It was the best moment ever.

Our evening celebration with family and friends was upbeat and happy, disrupted only by the smoke wafting out from under a guest's blue wool blazer, which had been ignited by a low-lying candle. The party didn't miss a beat, even as a chunk of his blazer's polyester lining melted onto the rug—a forever reminder of an unforgettable day.

Many years ago, on February 16, we began a journey filled with laughter, love, and adventure…followed later that year by a beautiful baby boy. It was a perfect wedding, when everything went very wrong but also very right.

IT'S ALL IN HOW YOU SAY IT

The young kid at the grocery-store checkout had just finished ringing up the avocados, pigs in a blanket, and bag of egg noodles—the ones without the egg yolks. Norman, as his Food Tiger badge indicated, seemed uncomfortable as he shifted back and forth from foot to foot. I was wondering if he might have a bit of an itch that he was dying to scratch but had thought better of it because his mother had probably said, "Norman, don't touch yourself in public!"

Norman looked across the conveyer belt, staring at me directly in the eye through my bifocals. He said without hesitation, "And your senior citizen's discount today is three dollars and forty-three cents."

Whoa! Wait just one minute, Norman-with-an-itch. Who said anything about my being a senior citizen? I sure don't recall you asking my age or asking if I was over sixty but possibly under one hundred. That itchy cashier kid had said "senior citizen" like it was obvious, as if the whole grocery store knew for certain that I was a senior citizen. You'd think I had it tattooed on my forehead, for heaven's sake. That boy didn't even allow for the possibility that maybe, just maybe, I was a few weeks or even months under the "age of seniority," whatever that was in this store.

Exactly what age are we talking about, Norman? Age sixty-five, when Medicare kicks in? Age sixty-two, when you can start collecting back your forty years of social-security contributions? Age sixty, when you sound a whole lot older than you do at fifty-nine? Did you learn to guess ages at the state fair and then hand out stuffed toy giraffes when you got it wrong, Norm? Maybe you owe me a giraffe.

Ever think of that, Norm?

I mean, Norman had to be making a wild guess based on...what? My grayish hair mottled with some dark hairlets? My very slightly sagging turkey neck? The hot coral lipstick bleeding into my lip creases? I mean, those things can happen at forty-nine or fifty-three or fifty-seven, can't they? These are not legal evidence of age that Norman should use to certify me as senior. Shouldn't I have to present a special card declaring "I'm a senior" if I am one?

I wanted to scream, "Hey, look at the facts, Norman. I have a paying job, and I have a kid completing four and a half years of college. So how can you, a young whippersnapper, know for sure that I'm a senior citizen? And for the record, the name Norman sounds much older than

Diane, so maybe you should get the discount too, based on your old name, Norm."

I just don't know what they teach cashiers in cash-register school about good customer relations, but I can assure you that Normie must have snoozed through that lesson. Does he not get it that women are very sensitive about their age, their looks, and how well their eighty-dollar-per-ounce antiaging cream is working? The question that was on my mind, forcing me to bite my tongue until it bled, was this: How old did Norman think I was?

I faced every woman's difficult dilemma. If I asked Norm how old he thought I was, just to satisfy my vanity and curiosity, he might guess older than I really was. Then I would feel depressed, compelled to get TV's "Lifestyle Lift," and spend all our retirement savings to look non-senior-like, which would then prevent us from going on that RV vacation to Yellowstone that Honey has been dreaming about. But I just couldn't face the tourists in the RV park looking older than I was, now could I? Norman really opened a can of marital worms.

I'd bet my last buck that Norm would even say to a woman with a tubby tummy, "When is the baby due?"—which any man worth his whiskers knows not to ask, unless the woman is humming lullabies or is in labor in the breakfast-cereal aisle.

So here's my advice to Norman on the topic of senior citizens: When in doubt, leave it out. To the next young-ish "old lady" who approaches your cash register, say, "It's too bad you don't qualify for the senior citizen's discount, ma'am—you would save three dollars and forty-three cents."

At this point she'd happily proclaim, "But I do qualify, Norman—I really do. I know it's hard to believe, but see my license?" She'd push the card under his nose. He would then subtract $3.43 from her bill, and she'd walk out of the store with a spring in her step because Norman-with-the-itch thought she was much younger than she really was.

You see, Norman, we'd still get to the bleeping $3.43 discount, but by playing this little game with a woman my age, you'd have a friend and a customer for life.

It's all in how you say it, Norm. Pass it on.

THE RED SHOES

With twenty minutes to go before my airplane boarding call, I figured a trip to the restroom would be wise, so I hustled down the corridor, knowing time was tight. A quick jog to the right, and I was heading to the bathroom stall. Thank goodness—no line.

I sat down to do my business, then sat and sat some more. I stared down at my beautiful cranberry-red shoes, which perfectly matched my cranberry-red purse, making me a freak of fashion, given that color matching is so out of style. I really do know this fashion rule, just for the record, but I don't care.

I wished I had a book to read, as I believed this would have distracted me from my bathroom business and maybe nudged things along. Hmmm. I looked through my purse for something to read but found nothing. Ho hum.

Just then another woman arrived and sat down one stall to the left. It was quiet over there—she seemed to be doing the waiting game too. Must be something in the airport water. I noticed that she was wearing black loafers, which no other woman has owned since about 1982. This woman needs help from Stacy and Clinton, I thought. They would certainly throw her footwear in that trash can on *What Not to Wear*, saying, "Even your grandmother wouldn't be seen in these clodhoppers." Stacy and Clinton can be so ruthless but so right.

Another woman then entered the stall to my right, wearing large white sneakers. Poor thing—cranberry-red shoes would never come in her size. Women sure have big feet these days.

As I stared at her shoes, I started to feel very uneasy. My eyes darted to the black loafers in the stall on the left and then back to the supersize sneakers on the right. A sick feeling started in the pit of my stomach and migrated to my face, which became red and flushed.

Oh my heavens! Tell me this isn't true...tell me I am not sitting on a toilet in the men's restroom! Tell me, instead, that I am sitting beside big-footed women with no sense of foot fashion. I swear I will stop stealing my husband's pretzels if this sick feeling will just go away.

I thought about my stall mates sitting so quietly, so deceptively. No comments like "Hey, buddy—whazzup with the red shoes and purse?" Why couldn't they be normal men and call it like they see it?

And exactly where were all the men when I wandered into this men's ladies' room? Did I not read the gender sign before I entered? Did I miss seeing some masculine-type people when I walked into this forbidden domain? What did it matter now anyway? It was too late to rewrite history—I just had to get out of this mess. If I made a dash for it, maybe I could get out of the restroom before my stall mates emerged.

I carefully opened the stall door and looked out at a row of urinals, previously hidden behind a wall when I entered this illicit space. Incredibly, there was still not a single man in this restroom aside from my big-footed pals, who, as a side note, were still laboring in their stalls. They really need to eat a bit more roughage and fiber, I thought, but decided against offering them nutritional advice. Instead, I grabbed my cranberry-red purse, stared straight ahead, and made a break for the hallway, where I slipped anonymously into the rush-hour crowd. I quickly ran to my boarding area, fearing the potty police would catch me and force me into a do-over, this time in the women's restroom.

Three days later, when I had recovered from my trauma, I told my Love God about my adventure. I had just related the part about the black loafers when he said, "Please don't tell me you were in the men's restroom." Ah, the joy of being married for so many years.

Because of this bathroom blooper, I have learned to follow three simple steps when nature calls in a public place:

1. I now double-check the restroom door sign before I enter, particularly those signs in foreign languages or with precious but confusing cartoon gender symbols.
2. I read the sign again, pause, reread it, and proceed carefully.
3. As I enter the restroom, I look for signs of male life in case I slipped up on steps one and two.

My new restroom approach is working like a charm. Men, you are safe. For now.

CONFESSIONS OF A LIPSTICK ADDICT

Every Saturday morning I go to my weight-loss group to weigh in and face the music. Some of you may know the group I'm talking about—the one where you weigh in, express shock that your weight loss wasn't more because you ate like a rabbit, for heaven's sake, and then someone tells you how well you did that week, whether you lost two ounces or two pounds. I know, because I have lost both amounts.

Last week was a three-ounce loss, the equivalent of five shrimps. My loss barely registered on the scale, let alone in the mirror. Will clothes hang more loosely because I have slimmed down by five shrimps? I think not.

While I was staring miserably at my scorecard, the woman beside me leaned over and said, "I really like that lipstick you're wearing." I felt a surge of joy come over me.

Even though I had lost only three ounces, my lips received an honorable mention.

"Thank you so much," I sputtered. "I have actually worn this color for twenty-five years." I was about to continue in glorious detail about the other seventy-four lipsticks currently in my bathroom drawer, but the woman turned away from me like I had escaped from the home, apparently more interested in the presentation on zucchini than in my soliloquy on lipstick.

Oh my gosh. I just admitted out loud that I've worn this shade of lipstick for twenty-five years.

I would like to clarify, for the record, that I have optimistically bought over four hundred tubes of other lipsticks since 1985, of which only about thirty have been Revlon's Hot Coral 712. I keep trying to update myself, but once spring comes, I burst into 712 again. I also love Revlon lipsticks 720, 725, and 675 as well as my newest, Cha Cha Cherry 626. I buy other brands and colors, but they bleed, rub off, or change color.

OK, I confess I'm a lipstick addict. I wear lipstick all the time, except when I'm sleeping, although one time after a big night out when I had one too many "iced teas," I fell asleep with my face paint on and awoke the next morning fully made up, sporting Revlon's Love That Red 725. I can say unashamedly that I've never looked more polished at seven in the morning.

When did my addiction begin? It goes back to the first lipstick my mom and I bought at the local drugstore when I was thirteen. It was called "shrimp bisque," and it was in a fancy white-and-gold tube. If anyone else can remember the color of her first lipstick from fifty-plus years ago, I will happily share my spot on the podium in the Lipstick Hall of Fame.

Since buying that first tube, I've purchased lipsticks ranging from the frosted white lipsticks of the sixties to the brownish-plum colors of the eighties, which my Love God said make my lips look like they are "cyanotic"—in other words, "blue lips that look dead." I dumped those lipsticks fast.

I'm aware that the current trend is to more neutral, natural lipsticks, and I have twenty-five tubes of proof that I have tried to duplicate Jennifer A.'s looks many times. I have resigned myself to the fact that this is not achievable on me, so I just wear whatever lipstick makes me happy, whether it's in or out of style.

My reputation for colorful lipsticks follows me everywhere. A friend, whom I hadn't seen in years, recently saw my picture and said the first thing she recognized about me was my lipstick. Although I'm sure the comment was made teasingly, I was secretly pleased that my lipstick received a callout after all this time.

Even in my family of five women, I'm pretty much the lipstick expert. Recently my sister Wendy called to ask me the color of the lipstick I'd once recommended. I instantly suggested Pink in the Afternoon 415 without hesitation, adding that Wink for Pink 616 would be a fabulous backup shade. Who else would know their lipstick numbers off by heart?

My friend Leigh Ann complimented me on my favorite Hot Coral 712 one day. In the blink of an eye, I handed her a brand-new tube from my private stock. Over the next week, she received three compliments, including one right after she'd eaten lunch, which all women know is the real test of a lipstick's worthiness.

Besides Leigh Ann and that woman in my weight-loss group, there was also a girl at the drugstore and a woman at Walmart, who said they loved my hot coral lips. This makes a grand total of five very tasteful people who have loved my lipstick.

Now if I could just lose more than five shrimps on my next weigh-in, my lips *and* I will both be winners.

FORTY WRONG ANSWERS

The dreaded meet-the-teacher night had arrived. Torture by tickling would have been a lot more fun than meeting the teacher of our youngest offspring. Our fifth-grade son was a parent's delight—and a teacher's nightmare. He was always dreaming about that winning goal in the final game; always staring out the window, wanting to play baseball on a warm, sunny day; or clowning with the other kids who'd cover their mouths to stifle their laughter.

I didn't want to start this delicate conversation by airing my concerns over the young man's recently failed math test. Instead, I'd start slowly and gently, build up to my primary concern, and then end on a high note by recognizing the teacher's much-appreciated teaching methods. I would leave her feeling good about, and maybe even fond of, our progeny. My teacher-talk strategy was all set, and I was off to school to be Mom of the Year.

I strutted down the hall, rehearsing my concerns and hoping to find a way to make bad news sound better. I walked into the classroom, with the teacher meeting me in the middle.

"Good to meet you, Mrs. Pascoe. I've been looking forward to meeting the woman behind that boy."

Oh geez. Was there a hidden message in that remark, or was I just a tad sensitive? He's our fourth child, so we've had a bit of experience meeting teachers, and it has rarely gone well.

I recovered quickly. "Very nice to meet you too, Miss Davis," I said as I plopped myself onto a student's chair, fearful that it would break or that I wouldn't be able to get up without an assist from a construction crane.

The teacher lobbed the first volley. "I'm concerned about his knowledge of the multiplication tables, Mrs. Pascoe. Braden doesn't seem to have mastered them yet." *Yup. Teacher, 1; Mom, 0.*

But I was ready. "I've really been working on math drills with him because I know how important math is, Miss Davis." I was usually much wittier than this, but I was practicing being humble, as I thought it would be useful at some point.

In truth, my son and I have been rehearsing multiplication tables whenever we drive to school, hockey, or the grocery store. We practice before, during, and after dinner. I sneak math questions in whenever I can. If he plays my math game, he gets to play hockey. Every child has his or her currency. His happens to be a puck.

It was my turn to volley. "Miss Davis, I brought Braden's recent math test. You may recall that he got zero out of forty on this multiplication test in which he had to multiply three numbers by three numbers. This math mark seems oddly low—even a broken clock is right twice a day."

Maybe a bit of cute humor would keep her from becoming defensive and annoyed, I thought.

She picked up the test and stared at it, as though she couldn't recall marking forty red Xs on the page.

"You see, Miss Davis, it appears that he has right justified each row of multiplication rather than shifting one column to the left with each new row, so of course the answers will be wrong. He was probably not paying attention when you taught him this step." I was trying to be really kind. It was her first year of teaching, after all. But honestly, how could she not see the keep-to-the-right methodology he used?

"Yes, that is odd looking, for sure," she admitted. "I see what you mean. His actual multiplication looks correct. I'll reteach that lesson tomorrow just to be sure everyone understands."

Bingo! Now she's cooking! See, it takes two to create this math mess, missy. He isn't perfect, but he isn't the village idiot either. A daydreamer on occasion but smart, very smart. Teacher, 1; Mom, 1.

Now that the score was even, I was eager to make peace. I congratulated Miss Davis for implementing the "star" program by which the students could earn gold, silver, or blue stars for doing well on assignments and tests.

I mean, who doesn't love an incentive program to reward good student behaviors? I was sure that our son must have been at the top of the class in earning stars. Not a day went by when he didn't tell me about the stars he'd earned— mostly gold stars, in fact. What mother wouldn't have been thrilled to give her offspring some extra privileges, such as joining the lacrosse team, renting some videos, or going out for pizza? I couldn't have been prouder of the little man.

"Miss Davis, I just wanted to tell you how great it has been to see Braden so charged up by your star program," I gushed. "It's really motivating him, and he loves it. It's just the best thing that, that..."

I paused to give her a chance to jump in and praise my wunderkind, to tell me he really was a star, a leader, a whiz kid, except for that little multiplication test mishap, which was a glitch that we could forget about.

But the teacher's face did not move. There was no smile, no nod, no flicker of agreement with my assess-ment of my son's educational achievements. She looked like a stone face on Mount Rushmore with pink lipstick. This wasn't going like I thought it would. As I was trying to understand what was happening, the fog slowly started to lift.

"Oh my gosh—there is no star program, is there?" I asked softly. My world was collapsing. *Teacher, 2; Mom, 1.*

"No, there isn't a star program—never was. Perhaps your son was thinking about a star program from grade two or three."

Perhaps he wasn't thinking that at all, Miss Davis. Perhaps, just perhaps, the little weasel was thinking that his gullible mother would love to hear about such successes and would give him carte blanche to get anything his little heart desired. Just wait until I get home. This score won't last long. Son, 3; Mom, 0.

Incensed, I hightailed it out of the school as fast as my legs would carry me. While driving home, I rehearsed my conversation with that little Duke of Deception. I stomped into the house, searching room to room. I found our son watching videotapes of his hockey career, which was a good thing, since it was about to end.

"Braden, I met Miss Davis today, and she told me there is no star program and never was. Why did you tell me there was a star program?"

Unbelievably, he didn't retreat. "I know there isn't a star program, but I *wanted* there to be one!" In what kind of fantasyland did that boy live?

"But every day you made up all these stories about the stars you'd earned! Those were lies, son!" Lying was a felony in our house; doing poorly on a math test was a misdemeanor. Time for action.

"Not only did you lie about the star program, but I heard that you didn't tell the truth to one of your hockey friends. This must stop now, son. I'd like you to go in your room and to write an essay about why you lie."

Thirty minutes later he emerged with his essay. "I lie so I can look better than I am." *Ouch.* He then went on to describe more about this sad state of affairs—such amazing self-awareness at his young age.

Then came his revenge. "And another thing—you shouldn't say you don't want to be my mother!"

"Correction, son. I said I wasn't *proud* to be your mother when I found out you invented the star program."

"Well, I'm mad, and I'm not going to eat dinner tonight, Mom! I sure hope you're happy now!"

"OK—it's your choice, son."

He paused as he contemplated the consequences of his declaration. Had he gone too far?

"What's for dinner tonight, anyway?"

My boy was back, new and improved.

MUSTARD IS NOT AN
APHRODISIAC

While browsing the Internet, looking for news on banishing belly fat, I happened to read that men's favorite time for coochie coo is in the morning, while women's favorite time is 11:00 p.m. on Saturday night. And of course, I believe everything I read on the Internet.

So, one Saturday night, not surprisingly at 11:00 p.m., Honey and I were happily doing our thing when I began to feel a cramp in my left leg. He probably thought I was just being frisky, given that earlier in the evening, he'd spoiled me with a McDonald's chocolate-dipped ice-cream cone.

Be assured, it isn't easy to focus on love when your leg is in spasm, contorting into an abstract sculpture. I tried to ignore the cramp and seriously focus. Really, I did. I even straightened my leg and curled up my toes to try to shake the cramp while at the same time making little noises that would indicate I was still alive and fully engaged in our amorous efforts.

The straightening and curling technique didn't work, however, so at my wit's end, I blurted out that I had to get up because of the leg-cramp thing and that if he could just hold that thought, I'd be right back. I started walking briskly across the carpet to work out the cramp. Back and forth, back and forth. I glanced over lovingly at Honey, who was still waiting patiently.

But the cramp wouldn't go away. So, in a moment of desperation, I fled to the kitchen to grab a bottle of French's classic yellow mustard because I had read—on the Internet, of course—that it would relieve all forms of leg cramps. I gulped a heaping tablespoon of mustard, and with its scent still on my breath, I jumped back into our love nest in a last-ditch effort to restore that special feeling we almost had.

No, sirree. My Love God, not one to just lie around idly waiting for a leg to uncramp, was now watching his favorite TV show, *The Incredible Dr. Pol*, in which the vet was trying to deliver a calf that just wouldn't be born. It was stuck. The love nest, it seemed, had turned into a barnyard.

Hoping to reignite that 11:00 p.m. spark, I moved closer to Honey for a little snuggle, but instead he mumbled, "Jeepers, you smell like a hot dog." The Internet had neglected to mention that mustard, in addition to being a cramp killer, was apparently also a romance destroyer. I lay there cramped and crushed.

Just as I was pondering a snappy wifely response, the stuck calf popped out, with Honey and Dr. Pol cheering it on. It seems I'd been replaced in Honey's affections by a cow in labor. Now cramp-free but dejected, I turned the TV off and then flopped over on my side to contemplate how the night had gone so wrong.

Or had it? Mustard can fix cramps, but luckily it can't cramp love. In the midnight darkness, Honey moved in close with his warm hand touching my back.

Game on.

THE DACHSHUND IS A DIVA

Our dachshund lay down on her side in the middle of the road, like a charred log with a leash attached.

"Come on, Carley, let's go." No movement. "Please, Carley. A car is coming. You have to move."

But the diva dachshund wouldn't budge.

With the car getting closer, I had to act. I picked Carley up in one swoop and started marching up the road, with Wyatt the Riot (a yellow Labrador retriever) leading the procession. I carried the diva for fifty yards and then plopped her down on her four-inch bowed legs—she was off and running. Another Carley moment had passed.

Flashback to two years earlier when Carley, then a one-year-old black dachshund from a local dog rescue, visited with Karen the dog walker while I was at work and Honey was working from home. That evening, as Honey clicked the TV remote, he said quietly, "The dog walker asked today if we would like a rescue dog—a little black dachshund."

"Let me think for a moment—*No!*" I barked, not believing he had the nerve to even suggest this. "One dog is quite enough, thank you."

"That's exactly what I told her," he huffed. "Not only that, Karen said the dog leaks—she piddles everywhere." We have replaced too many rugs for me to let this revelation go unnoticed.

"What was the dog's name, anyway?" I asked. I should at least know the name of the dog who came to our home, right?

"I think it was Victoria," Honey offered.

Hmmm. Nice name. "Are you sure?" I questioned, knowing he struggled with names, including my own, at times. "Could it be Olivia?" I suggested, picking a name that sounded as queenlike as Victoria.

"Could be," he said. Back to clicking the remote.

The next day I asked if Victoria-Olivia had visited again.

"No," said Honey, trying to end the conversation quickly, though these conversations have a way of continuing.

On Wednesday evening I asked if that little black doggie had visited again. Honey stared at me like I'd lost my mind. He knew that tone of voice from a conversation about fifteen years earlier, when I'd brought up the subject of perhaps having another child. The child whom we talked about somewhat abstractly is now more than twenty years old.

"But you said that the dog's parents were divorced, and they took her to the rescue. Who will look after her if she doesn't have a mother?" I asked worriedly. We agreed we should bring her for a sleepover to see how she meshed with Wyatt the Riot.

The following day Honey called and said, "Carley is coming next Monday for a sleepover."

"Who's Carley?"

"The dog."

"I thought it was Victoria-Olivia?"

"I was wrong," said my Love God. *Whoa! Should mark that on the calendar.*

He called me back at work to say the sleepover date wouldn't work for the rescue facility.

"Forget the sleepover then. Just tell the little wiener girl to pack up her purse and move in." I was clearly smitten with her, sight unseen.

He called back again and said, "Karen will drop Harley Jane by the house on Tuesday."

"Who is Harley Jane?"

"The dog." *Have we not had this conversation about the dog's name before, Honey?*

"What happened to Victoria-Olivia-Carley?"

"I was wrong." *Lordy, lightning really does strike twice. Buy a lottery ticket quick.*

Tuesday came and so did Victoria-Olivia-Carley-Harley Jane, just as promised. She took over the house, piddling at every warm greeting or touch of a hand. She weighed only thirteen pounds and looked too small to be called Harley Jane. To avoid confusing her, we stuck with the similar-sounding name, Carley.

Fast-forward a year. The little wiener had ballooned to a seventeen-pound sausage. On strict doctor's orders, she went on a diet during which she gained weight, reaching eighteen pounds. So the dog walker hooked Carley's leash to an energetic Yorkie named Rocky, who dragged Carley around the yard on a forced daily exercise program. Slowly her weight crept down to sixteen pounds.

Our little wiener girl is not perfect, however. One day she snuck out a door that had been left ajar and went missing for hours. We checked the lost-and-found dog listings online and discovered that a black dachshund had been found in a nearby subdivision on a resident's back porch. "Very friendly" was the description in the listing, a dead giveaway that it was our girl. When I finally caught up with her, the bow-legged opportunist had just finished her second meal with her newest family and was being carried around their house by their young daughter. Dumb like a fox, that wiener girl.

She still loves her treats and hates walking, particularly if she smells rain in the air. But Victoria-Olivia-Carley-Harley Jane-Carley, an affectionate and cuddly lap dog who smells like a Frito, is a part of this family till death do us part.

THE DAY I WAS FIRED

I'm going to be flat-out honest with you. I was fired once from a position I had always wanted. It was the supreme failure of my life to that point. I had no one else to blame, though goodness knows I tried. With this firing, I entered the Hall of Shame, where you get to ponder your failures for the rest of your life.

Being fired hasn't been my only failure, of course. Being divorced also suggests loser behavior, but I jointly own that one with my ex, Mr. Wrong, and as you'd probably guess, I believe he owns the bigger share of the blame. Well, that's my story, and I'm sticking to it.

When I first got the f-word from the boss, I was stunned. I was fired in front of my peers. I sobbed. It was my dream job because it possessed fame, glory, and prestige. I loved the position, though in retrospect, I was wholly unprepared for the responsibility, the technical requirements, and the spotlight it put me in.

I remember f-day like it was yesterday. I can vividly recall that my brown hair was cut in a bob, with crooked bangs sloping from left to right. I could imagine what the neighbors said: *Lordy, did that girl get her hair cut by the hairdresser or the dog groomer?* Even I, a four-year-old, knew I looked weird.

Yup—I was four years old when I was fired.

The nightmare happened when I was in the kindergarten rhythm band. I was usually relegated to banging two sticks together or clanging the triangle. I didn't like playing the sticks…it was like putting Baby in the corner. I wanted to be the lone glorious drum pounder or the tambourine shaker, not a crummy twig tapper.

Then one day my teacher, Miss Coyle, asked me if I'd like to be the band conductor. You know, like Ricky Ricardo or Mitch Miller. My flat chest puffed up; my shoulders went back. I was handed the baton, led up to the platform, and turned around to face my kindergarten band—a sea of hopeful faces staring at me.

Now this is the point at which it all started to go wrong. I had no idea what I was supposed to do with that flipping baton. I had seen Ricky and Mitch on TV, but with severe four-year-old performance anxiety, I couldn't recall if they twirled it, tossed it, or drew circles with it. I just stood there, baton arm frozen at my side, and started to cry.

Miss Coyle grabbed the baton and started waving it wildly, while the twig-tapping girls began banging their wooden instruments of musical torture. The tune ended, and I slipped away to my seat on the floor, head down, silent.

The next day the teacher called me up to the platform and handed me the baton once again. Oh good, a fresh start! But I still didn't know what to do with that darn baton. So I cried—again.

Then came the final insult. The teacher called on Raymond, who hadn't even learned how to tie his shoes yet, to take over my job. I had no warning, no probation. She just passed him *my* baton and asked me to sit down with the rest of the faceless, nameless stick bangers. Then Raymond started waving the baton just like I'd seen the conductors do on TV.

Please, Miss Coyle, I get it now!

I desperately tried to catch the teacher's eye to show her the light had finally come on. But she had eyes only for Raymond, leaving me in the corner with my sticks. I was yesterday's news.

For more than fifty years, I've been swinging that baton in my dreams to see if I could get it right. I can't read a musical note or carry a tune, and my pitch has been off since the birth of my first child. And no, I don't see the connection between birth and pitch either. Music was never going to be my career, so my baton failure was probably inconsequential in the scheme of things.

But here's the important stuff that I learned in Miss Coyle's class:

- I learned that firing is just the umpire telling you that you lost the game when all along you were playing poorly and probably knew how it would end anyway.
- I learned that with a bit of help, people could learn to do their jobs much better.
- I learned that career success is possible when your career goals fit your strengths. In other words, don't try to swim upriver—that's for fish.
- I learned that pain dulls with time, and humor carries the day.
- I learned that failures are where life's lessons are learned, so celebrate failure as a character builder.

See—I really did get it, Miss Coyle.

I'D LOSE MY HEAD IF IT
WEREN'T ATTACHED

Don't you hate that sinking feeling you get when your (*name of your lost item*) isn't where you thought it was? I have more experience with this subject than I care to divulge, but I will anyway. Getting it off my chest will be cheaper than psychotherapy, I figure.

One day I left my red wallet on the roof of the car when I was pumping gas because I couldn't hold the gas pump handle and my wallet at the same time, now could I? I drove off with that little red thing sitting on my car roof. Nobody waved furiously at me, so I drove home thirty-two miles, none the wiser. When I looked for my credit card two hours later to order something online that I didn't need, you guessed it—no red wallet.

I steeled myself to confess to Honey about my/our little problem, and of course, he rolled his eyes and told me I'd lose my head if it weren't attached.

Honey suggested that we drive back thirty-two miles to the gas station where I last had my wallet in case it had fallen on the ground somewhere.

This, I thought, will be the longest, quietest thirty-two minutes of my life.

But as there was no other way out of this purgatory, I buckled up, cranked up the radio, and hummed along, off-key as always. At the gas station, I asked the attendant if she'd seen a red wallet, but she hadn't, so we drove back to the highway while I looked in the gutters and on the road—but alas, no flash of red leather. My wallet was gone forever, and I now needed to replace all ID, credit cards, and even my customer card for Bare Minerals makeup. I would have to start over, collecting those little hole punches to get one free mineral makeup for every one thousand purchases.

Three months passed; then one day my phone rang. A man asked if I'd lost a red wallet—he said he'd found it on the side of the highway when he was picking up garbage. I met him at McDonalds, recovered my wallet, and thanked him profusely for his kindness.

See, Honey, I didn't really lose it because I have it, right?

Fast-forward two weeks, when I was in Oklahoma, getting ready to leave for the airport. I had double-checked to be sure I had my ticket, cell phones—but wait…where was my pink phone? I saw my red work phone buried in my purse but not my pink personal phone. I also saw Honey's face in my mind, mouthing the words, "You'd lose your head, blah, blah, blah."

I have been scarred for life by his declarations about my head.

I rushed back to the hotel, got a new room key, and went to room 310, noting that the sheets had been pulled off the bed for washing. I looked everywhere but couldn't find the dang pink phone; I was starting to sweat—I had a plane to catch. But then I had a brainstorm: I'd use my red phone to call my pink phone, which may have been hiding somewhere in the room. I entered my phone number and heard a faint ring, ring, ring. I tried to follow the sound but couldn't pinpoint it. So I went into the hall and called my pink phone again. The ringing was a bit closer. At the end of the hall, I spotted a laundry cart. *Hmmm.* The ringing got louder as I approached the cart. I called out for the cleaning lady, and she appeared, speaking Spanish. This was not good. I pointed at the ringing cart and told the *seniorita cleania* that *mia phona* was in her *cartia*. As she pulled the bedsheets out one by one, my pink phone suddenly popped up.

Thank goodness. I'd just avoided the "you'd lose your head" lecture by a bedsheet.

The next day, when I was buying a gift for a friend with my credit card, the clerk asked for my license. I pored through all twelve compartments of my purse. No license!

I rushed home and went through all my clothes worn in the past three days. Still no license.

In desperation, I braced myself and asked Honey if he had seen my license. He gave me *the look*, followed predictably by comments about *my head*. Oh yes, I did find the card...in the makeup bag in my purse, right beside my hot coral lipstick. Go figure.

"Life is just very complicated," I said to console myself. So much to keep track of, so many possible hiding places. I decided I just needed to relax, have some iced tea, then sit down on the sofa to read the paper.

Suddenly I was jolted back to reality. Where the heck did my glasses go? I was quite certain they were right there on the table beside the chocolate ice-cream sandwich wrapper.

As I went to the kitchen to search for the wayward specs, I caught a glimpse of myself in the mirror with the lost glasses perched right on top of my head—which, just to set the record straight, was still very much attached.

My head is apparently the *only* thing I haven't lost.

NICE PACKAGE

One eye opens. The other eye, buried in pillow fluff, reluctantly follows. They merge lazily, looking toward the hotel room alarm clock, which reveals it is 7:06 a.m. and time to roll.

There's so much to do. Shower, dry hair, paint face, get dressed, and pack. If we expect to get home by noon, we need to get going. I'll leave Honey to sleep a bit because his morning routine is very quick—shower, shave, brush teeth, get dressed—takes twelve minutes, fifteen minutes at the most, if he flosses.

I'm feeling very tired this morning, but I keep going, shampooing my hair until the water runs clear. Wash myself from face to feet. Blow-dry gray hairlets. Spray them into submission. Swish on makeup. I'm almost done—just need to brush my teeth.

I grab the little red-and-white toothpaste tube and drop a generous blob of toothpaste on my toothbrush. Swish, swash, swish. Wait a minute—where's the mint taste? The taste is yucky—like grease without the bacon bits. *What exactly is this stuff?*

I reach for my eyeglasses to see which offending concoction I'm using. Oh my gosh—it says it's "Cortisone Cream for Itchy Skin." That would be the same cortisone steroid that is also used in hemorrhoid ointments. I spit it out instantly and then hunt down the red-and-white tube of minty toothpaste, which is still lying at the bottom of my makeup bag. Brush my teeth again. Real toothpaste tastes so much better.

This toothpaste error has thrown me off my game. Maybe that's why I still feel so sleepy. I vow that this cortisone-toothpaste fiasco will remain my little secret. No point in giving Honey more reason to think my faculties are declining. He'll make my itsy-bitsy faux pas a much bigger deal than it really is. Just because his name slips my mind from time to time is no reason to question my mental acuity, is it?

I snap out of my steroid stupor. I'm ready to go, but my Love God is still lying in bed in his red boxer shorts that have a Christmas present and "Nice Package" displayed on the rear. The back of his frayed gray pajama T-shirt lists the names of all the Carolina Hurricanes hockey players who were on the 2006 Stanley Cup team. That was ten years ago. *The game is so over, and so is the T-shirt, Honey.*

I don't understand why my Love God is moving so slowly this morning. If he's sick, I may have to drive the whole way home myself, which would be horrible. I usually fake being asleep when it's my turn to drive. I've also been known to yawn incessantly while at the wheel until Honey finally tells me to pull over, and then wham, bam—I'm a passenger again.

I give it another try. "We need to get going—*chop, chop, Honey!* We'll never be home by noon unless we get going right now!"

He slowly rolls over in bed and lifts his pillow-wrinkled face, staring at me like he knows about my secret cortisone-toothpaste mishap.

"What are you doing?" he says in a drowsy voice.

By now, Honey is getting on my nerves, which have been frazzled since I ingested the cortisone. I don't have the time or the energy to play Honey-Di word games. *It is not a new process, Honey. We get up and get ready every single morning of the year, so get moving!*

The next words out of his mouth are as frightening as anything he has ever said to me. "What are you doing out of bed? It's one thirty-five a.m."

Whaaaat! I look over at the clock, which really does say 1:35 a.m. He's not teasing me. But wasn't it 7:06 a.m. when I got up? I remember looking at the clock and it said… wait, did it say 1:06 a.m. or 7:06 a.m.? What a difference a little horizontal line makes. I'm now standing here in the middle of the night, having showered, washed my hair, and dressed, with lips screaming Revlon Hot Coral 712.

I quickly assess my choices: I can undress, remove my makeup, and go back to sleep until the real 7:00 a.m. and then have my third shower in twenty-four hours, or I can sleep sitting upright to preserve my coiffure and avoid that third shower and shampoo. I opt for the sleep-and-shower-again routine because I find it hard to sleep sitting up, unless I'm on an airplane with my eyes shut and mouth open, snoring.

I bury my head in the pillow and try to resume sleeping. My eyeglasses are nearby so that I can read the clock clearly. The minty toothpaste is on the counter, and the cortisone cream is out of sight.

Bring on the morning—I am *so* ready.

I'M FAT, FED UP, AND FIGHTING BACK

It was New Year's Day, and I could hardly move. I wasn't paralyzed, nor did I have a broken leg. I was fat, over-weight, chubby, fluffy, pudgy—pick your poison.

My weight had started to climb at Halloween, the beginning of the festive grazing season, reaching a high on New Year's Day. My clothes were too tight, even the stretchy ones. It was clear I had to get focused, get fit, and do something fast.

I frantically searched online for a local weight-loss pro-gram. You know—the one where you count points and get weighed at a weekly meeting. Of course, leaders in that program never use the word "fat," but I'm comfortable with the f-word. It is what it is, and I own it. Using a pret-tier word won't make me feel any slimmer.

The morning of my first meeting arrived. I showered, brushed my hair, and put on makeup—I wanted to look polished even if I looked plump. Then I donned a light, gauzy tunic in the hopes of minimizing my weight on the scale.

Sitting anxiously in my car outside the weight-loss-program office, I finally mustered up the courage to walk through the door. I wondered if I would have to speak at each meeting: *Hi. My name is Diane, and I've lost only five ounces this week, but I can explain why if you have an hour or so.*

I was also imagining the meeting wrap-up: the group leader would total all the weight lost that week; then we'd sing "We Are the Champions," followed by "Kumbaya," and then we'd have a group hug. *Heaven help me.*

I got out of my car and hesitantly entered the office. An assistant greeted me enthusiastically.

"Hi, there. Is this your first meeting?"

"Yes, ma'am. It is."

The conversation in my head was quite different, however: *Ma'am, could you please lower your voice just a smidgen? I'm trying to be invisible so nobody looks at me. I'm only here because my clothes don't fit, and I have nothing in my closet to wear. I'm sure I'll feel chattier when I'm a bit thinner.*

But being polite, I instead smiled weakly, handed her my credit card, and got on the scales as instructed. I removed my sweater, watch, and shoes in front of the growing line of people ready to weigh in. I wished they had a private weigh-in booth where I could lean a bit to the left to try to affect the scales, or shed all my clothes to shave two or three offending ounces off my weight. The bubbly assistant then handed back my record book showing my weight. I nervously peeked at it. *Oh lordy: Where did that weight come from? I will need to lose forty pounds. Well, maybe more like fifty pounds. OK, OK—sixty pounds.*

The meeting was starting, so I put my record book away and anxiously slipped into a chair at the back of the group-therapy room. Over the next thirty minutes, I learned that caramels don't have the same points as carrots. There was much talk about veggies, whole wheat, and fiber, but not a positive word about McYummy's happy meals or warm sausage biscuits. The meeting message was clear: my meals had to undergo big changes.

But fluffy people often come in pairs, it seems, so I was thrilled when Honey decided to join me on my journey so that we wouldn't have to cook separate meals. He is my Love God, maker of steamed veggies and griller of fish. Gone from our diets are the three Cs: cookies, crispy chicken skin, and cheese. We have swallowed the Kool-Aid (sugar-free, of course) and are totally with the program. Even the dogs have lost weight. No more cheese chunk treats—they get watermelon wedges and baby carrots now.

Life has changed in many other ways since my New Year's meltdown. Most importantly, I have lost weight, just as the leaders said I would if I changed my lifestyle. My clothes are no longer tight—they are in fact much too big! I even look forward to my weekly group meetings, when my new friends and I can share our successes and slipups.

I guarantee my struggle is not over, but I now know what works and what doesn't.

The festive grazing season starts again soon, and I'll be ready to fight temptation when the Halloween treats appear because I have learned five important things in my weight-loss group:

- To eat well but to eat less.
- To eat until I'm satisfied, not until it hurts.
- To love the food I eat but to change the food I love.
- Each of us is stronger as part of a group than as individuals.
- New clothes are the best revenge.

"Good night, Honey. Love you!"

"Honey, are you still awake? Was that chicken thigh three points or four?"

THIS WAS NOT THE PLAN

Honey and I are planners by nature. We develop a plan; we work the plan. Quite simple, really.

Four years ago we had a plan to start scouting the coastal area for a retirement community. We would then sell the big house with the mortgage, build a small but perfect cottage home, and lie on the beach all day. We quickly found the ideal spot, bought the land, and had a sign plopped on it that said, "Future Home of the Pascoe Family." Please note that the word "future" is very open ended.

Buoyed by the vision of us frolicking in the ocean waves, I decided it was time to retire with Honey, who had just left an uninspiring sales job. I gave my notice at work, purged the house of junk, and listed it with a real estate firm that helps owners sell their houses by themselves. Honey and I've always sold houses ourselves. We are do-it-yourself people. Thrifty, some might say. Others might call us cheap.

But then Honey threw a wrench into the retirement plan. He decided to unretire and take a job at a local sportsmen's store until we moved to the small but perfect coastal house. I couldn't keep up with him. *Were we working, unemployed, or retiring?* I was beginning to think that retirement and unemployment looked much the same.

Fast-forward to six months after the date we bought the property. The big house had not sold. It had been cleaned 183 times but still had not sold. I'd baked twenty-four dozen cookies to impress the house gawkers who, apparently, just wanted to see how well I could make a bed with no lumps in it. Many compliments—but no offers and no nibbles—so we took it off the market temporarily until conditions improved. The "Future Home of the Pascoe Family" had moved much farther into the future than we'd hoped.

It looked like we needed to retire the retirement plan. So I halfheartedly applied for a temporary part-time job, and as bad luck would have it, the recruiter called me to come in for an interview the next day. Recruiters never call except when you don't want them to. My wonderful, stay-at-home life was clearly at risk.

The next day I went to meet the recruiter. She said I was lucky—a temporary *full-time* job was available that might suit me. The recruiter would send my résumé to the employer to gauge their interest. "It could even become permanent!" she gushed.

Oh darn, not *permanent*, I thought. Didn't she understand that I was older, blissful, relaxed, and wanted to be mostly retired, not mostly working? Maybe the company representative would do the math and figure out I was about 105, but of course, being politically correct, she'd tell the recruiter I was "too this" or "not enough that."

Out of nowhere I heard myself say that I'd meet with the company's hiring managers the next day if she really wanted me to. My desire to please was going to cause me a problem if I didn't have a backup strategy to avoid getting this job. I decided that I would not be charming, and I would wear the brightest lipstick I owned, which would scare anyone under age forty. I'd be sure to eat broccoli for lunch so there would be some green specks in my teeth. Then I'd laugh like a hyena so they would roll their eyes and want to end the interview. I'd give very truthful answers instead of enhanced responses designed to make me seem fabulous and clever. I'd then be rejected and remain retired.

The next day I interviewed with two lovely but unsuspecting women, who believed they were interviewing someone who truly wanted the job. But once again my plan failed—the recruiter called to say they loved me and asked if I could start right away. However, when the recruiter told me the salary, it prompted another brilliant escape plan—I'd demand more money, more vacation days, a shoe allowance, free chocolate kisses, a crown—you get the picture. I'd hoped that this approach would end absurd talk of any job offer. And just to add further drama to the negotiation, I informed the recruiter that she had only seven minutes to call me back, as I was about to walk through the gates of the US Open at Pinehurst, and it was a no-cell-phone zone.

Suddenly I heard *ringy ding ding.* The recruiter was calling me back after she talked with the company reps. "No problem," she bubbled. "They're fine with everything you asked about."

No, no, no! This was not my plan at all! I wanted to be retired on the beach in my black-and-white-patterned bathing suit similar to that of a Holsten cow that my kids moo at. I paused, trying to think of a clever comeback to the recruiter, but the fight had gone out of me. Three days later I started working full time—again. No more sleep-ins, no more beach-bunny dreams.

Here's what I learned from this experience: when Honey and I decided to retire, we should have made sure the old house *had already been sold* and the new perfect one built. Then we should have retired. The lawn sign would then have read "*New* Home of the Pascoe Family." No "*Future*" about it!

SAY NO TO IN-FLIGHT INTIMACY

As airline seats have become smaller and passengers' girths have expanded, airline flyers are increasingly putting their marriages at risk. I speak from experience because as a pudgy passenger, I almost had unplanned intimate relations on a recent flight, and it wasn't even with my Love God, Honey.

I'm grateful that I haven't yet had to ask for a seat-belt extender, but I might be asking for one soon if I don't start saying no to mayo and yes to lettuce. I dread the mere thought of having to say, "Yoo-hoo, missy, can you toss a seat-belt extender back to row twenty-three, 'cause I can't get this thing around my tumpa wumpa due to the extra mayo and cheese." All heads would turn to see if I am a full-figured woman, while the scrawny attendant would yell back, "Lady, we're out of extenders, so just suck it in, could you, please?" *Lordy, just let me die now.*

How is a woman like me supposed to fly in comfort, stay unwrinkled, and remain faithful to her Love God when the airline insists on making its passengers play footsie and armsie in such close quarters? The next thing you know, my seatmate and I will be playing spin the mini wine bottle on my folding table.

I count the rows ahead to see who my seatmate will be and pray that Mr. Big Mac, whom I see up ahead, isn't in row nine. *Let me see now....six, seven, eight, oh no...nine.* Geez, my seat is smack beside Mr. BM, who by now has made eye contact with me and is looking as scared as I am at the prospect of sharing a row. I'm no prize, but he makes me look like Twiggy. As I approach our row, he reluctantly extracts himself from his seat so I can squeeze by him and into the dreaded middle seat. A spot in cargo atop mountains of frozen luggage would be preferable to this unfortunate arrangement.

My portly pal sits back down, overflowing his seat, while I hug myself tightly into an egg-roll shape to avoid my arm touching his arm. I don't know him, and I'm certainly not married to him, so I don't want our body parts to get friendly. Even his leg is touching mine because his knees are spread about three feet apart, over the invisible line that defines my personal space.

This is intimacy without the fun.

I try to cross my legs tightly to squish myself in, but my butt starts to cramp from the tension. Mr. Big Mac then has the nerve to put his arm on *my* side of the armrest, which is for *my* arm per my airplane-ticket agreement. I have made a mental note to check the exact wording of that agreement, if I ever dislodge myself, so I can quote it to my next armrest-stealing seatmate.

This forced passenger intimacy could be avoided if all passengers were required to report their weight on the booking information. The computer would then seat corpulent customers between skinny passengers, who hopefully wouldn't be that annoyed about a little neighborly overflow, as they don't use all their space anyway. I'm thinking they could even be rewarded with a few extra airline points for their kindness because the airlines want all passengers to play nice in the air. Chubby, thin, chubby, thin. That's a seating arrangement that will surely prevent extramarital in-flight intimacy.

I would even offer my skinny seatmates my peanuts, pretzels, and cookies because I won't be eating them—I am planning to lose weight to avoid putting my marriage to Honey at risk because of in-flight shenanigans.

So hold the mayo and chuck the cheese; size really matters in an airplane.

CAN YOU MOVE IT?

Whump!

Our youngest son's feet shot straight out from under him on the driveway. His screech could have raised the dead as he landed heavily on his arm. I knew it would be just a matter of time before those roller skates betrayed him, causing bodily injury.

He raised his arm limply in front of me as he winced. The arm looked normal to me. "Can you move it?" I questioned, in my best nurse voice.

He nodded.

"Then you must have just bruised it—let's get some ice on it." No need to dwell on every childhood ache and pain, right?

The next morning before summer camp, he complained that his arm was sore and maybe he shouldn't go to camp.

"Can you move it?" I asked again, just to double-check that my diagnostic skills were intact. He nodded. "Then you're fine. Off to camp now."

My office phone rang at 2:00 p.m. It was the camp counselor.

"Your son just tripped over a tree root and fell on his sore arm. He says it really hurts."

Jeepers...can that boy not stay on his feet for just one day? Is he determined to torment me? I packed up some of my office work and headed for camp.

His Royal Shortness was sitting on a log, rubbing the offending arm. "It feels much better now, Mom," he said as I reflected on all the work I'd just left behind at the office to tend to an arm that felt much better.

"Can you move it?" I inquired, asking the only medical question I knew to ask in such circumstances. He nodded. "Well, good. It's fine then."

"Do you think I should play in the soccer game tonight?" he wondered.

"Of course," I replied, sensing the start of a pity party. "You can't let your team down just because your arm is a bit sore. A little pain never hurt anybody, son."

I continued lecturing as only a mother can, hoping to teach him the importance of biting the bullet, sucking it up, and all the other metaphors meant to make men out of boys. *That's my job, right?*

The game warm-up began with our man-boy goalie in place, stopping each ball with his left arm, while the impaired right arm lay limply at his side. I admit it looked kind of peculiar.

Just as I was pondering this odd-looking scene, a soccer-ball missile hit his dangling right arm. That would be the same arm that he had assured Nurse Mom he could move and that I had assured him is fine.

My Love God, who had remained silent on my medical diagnostic technique to that point, said impatiently, "Do you *think* you could take him to the hospital to have it checked?"

Jeepers! Did my Love God grow up under a mushroom? Did he not receive the same medical education from his parents that I had—that if an arm can move, it can't possibly be broken? Are we raising a marshmallow or a man-to-be? Is no one listening? The boy can move it! He said so himself!

By then it was clear that I'd need to prove the soundness of my medical advice with a four-hour wait in the emergency room. We sat and sat. They finally x-rayed the limb, which had been laying like a wet noodle on his lap.

"What do you think is wrong, Mom?"

Testing one last time that it really was a moveable limb, I asked, "Can you move it?" He nodded. I felt like I had been singing a refrain from a familiar song. "Then it's just a bad bruise, son."

The doctor appeared. "Mrs. Pascoe, your son has a broken arm and will need a cast on it for six weeks." His words pierced my heart.

"*Whaaat?*" I croaked. "But he can move it—isn't that the rule?"

Was my medical training flawed? Would child services be called and sentence me to baking brownies for the little man-boy whenever his stomach rumbled?

"Son, I am so sorry," I apologized. "I didn't know. Can you ever forgive me?"

"Sure, Mom—but can you please carry my backpack, shoes, coat, and books for me? I know it's heavy, but a little pain never hurt anybody."

Ouch.

THE SECOND-RUNNER-UP PROM PRINCESS

"Honey, did I ever tell you I was the second-runner-up prom princess at school?" I asked my Love God one Sunday afternoon.

Love God countered, "Did I ever tell you I started the milk program at school?"

Good lord! He had told me this at least 263 times, and anyway, he could hardly compare being a school milkman to my being a second-runner-up convent-school prom princess, now could he?

"Son, did *you* know I was a backup prom princess?"

My defenseless offspring had no time to get away. "Mom, it was a convent girl's school—that's just not right!"

He did have a point, however trivial.

This convent-school experience needs some background scene-setting. The uniform was a pea-green jacket with a matching skirt, which disobeyed all fashion rules. Black knee-high socks were forever at half-mast, like they were in mourning. I wore black Oxford lace-up shoes, which could inflict injury on any unwitting Romeo who was nutty enough to pursue me. To complete the school-girl look, I wore bubblegum-pink lipstick, hand-drawn eyebrows, and much-too-rosy circles on my cheeks. I think you get the picture.

The highlight of grade twelve was the prom, which brought on the twin towers of fear—what to wear and who I'd invite as my date. So when I heard that a friend had dumped her Mr. Not Quite Perfect, I called him quickly to seal the deal. He agreed, dreaming of a free meal and the chance to get a glimpse of his former girlfriend, who was going to the dance with a more perfect Mr. Perfect. I knew I was just the "transition girl," but he passed the breathing test, and besides, dates were hard to come by when you wore convent garb.

Now that the who-will-be-my-date issue was settled, only the dress dilemma needed attention. I could picture a purple formal frock with cut-in shoulders and a white Peter Pan collar—much like a Playboy bunny would wear but with a skirt attached for modesty. I finished this creation in a few nights of intense sewing.

Prom night arrived. Mr. Not Quite Perfect, who had enjoyed a few sips of high-octane Kool-Aid prior to the event, could not stop making goo-goo eyes at his ex-girlfriend while breathlessly proclaiming to me his desire to become a priest after playing professional hockey for a few years. Jeepers, I sure could pick winners.

A crowd started to gather in the gym under the basketball net. It was time to announce the prom queen. The band was playing as my hockey player-cum-priest swayed to the music, sipping from his flask of Kool-Aid while worshiping his ex, who admittedly looked "mahvelous" and tanned, with a skin-tight white dress and white chicklet teeth. In my mind's eye, I could see the crown on her head. Heck, *I* even voted for her. I popped another cookie in my mouth to celebrate my certain defeat.

The PA system crackled as the announcer said, "The second-runner-up prom princess is Diane Windsor!"

Good lord! You could have pushed me over with a bunny tail. The hockey player-cum-priest fell into a chair, overcome by his Kool-Aid, while I floated up to the podium to accept my flowers. Then they called the first runner-up, and lastly the queen. I heard not a thing. The sound of my name was still ringing in my ears.

The picture in the next evening's paper was proof to my disbelieving sisters that I, their Cinderella, was the spare to the heir, in case the queen had to be dethroned for cursing or whatever a queen gets dethroned for in a convent.

I know I can't put "second-runner-up prom princess" on a résumé or use it to secure a car loan, but I will forever know that, at least on that one night in grade twelve, I was sort of near-royalty. And by the way, I think I heard that Mr. Not Quite Perfect Hockey Player Priest Wannabe became an insurance salesman driving a Gremlin. *Woo-hoo.*

COLONOSCOPY CONFESSIONS

I want to let you in on a little secret. Procrastination has always been one of my secret joys, particularly when unpleasant activities are involved. Things will eventually get to me, of course, but until then, I enjoy putting things off. Except maybe for eating.

I happily delayed having that most "delicate" of all procedures—a colonoscopy—until the guilt finally caught up with me. It was well past the recommended time for that micro camera to peek in my pipeline to be sure everything was pretty and pink. I decided it was time to grow up and show up.

I made the appointment for April Fool's Day, which my Love God noted was perhaps a poor choice of dates. Would the doctor joke and tell me he thinks he just located my missing compact umbrella with the comfort handle? I tried not to be deterred by such unsettling thoughts and forged ahead.

I bought the prep materials and read the literature. No raw fruits or vegetables for five days, it said in bold letters. Without fruits and veggies, I'd be forced to eat chocolate, ice cream, and cookies. I practiced my excuses for my weekly weight-loss-program meeting: *it's not my fault...I had to eat chocolate for medical reasons. Honest.*

The rules of colonic photo sessions were clear: the day before the procedure, I was not supposed to eat at all, except for clear fluids that weren't red or purple, which just happened to be my two favorite beverage colors. I really didn't understand why I couldn't eat whatever I wanted, given that I was going to be drinking a liquid that apparently would create an internal tsunami that would wipe out all traces of food. But I followed the rules because I couldn't take a chance that the doctor would declare to everyone within earshot that he couldn't get his minicam past the chocolate kisses and meatballs.

The evening before the colonoscopy, I dutifully drank the salty lemonade-tasting mixture and then followed up with two sixteen-ounce water chasers. I jogged to the throne seven times before bed and once during the night. I repeated this satanic ritual in the morning; then Honey and I headed off to the clinic.

They were ready for me. With military precision I had visits from the anesthesiologist, the bummologist, and two female doctorologists, who praised my lipstick, my matching nails, and my eyeglasses, commenting on how very nicely I was put together. I was flattered but worried that their interest in fashion rather than medicine would distract them from my pipeline probe for which I had just swallowed thirty-two ounces of water and was about to burst.

Focus, ladies! Focus!

Honey commented that for the life of him, he couldn't figure out why I had on full face paint when I'd be unconscious and likely drooling. Logic has no place here, I tried to explain. I follow the same regimen every morning, without concern for what I'll be doing that day. I might be going to work or cleaning toilets or having the queen over for tea. Bottom line: I do my hair and makeup the same, regardless. Nobody should be forced to look at me au naturel—not even a bummologist, who likely wouldn't see much of my face from where he or she was sitting.

I was wheeled into the cold and dark peek-and-poke room, with Phil Collins warbling in the background. It was mildly comforting. The nurse told me I'd soon feel sleepy. Then I was gone. I woke up in what seemed like three minutes, talking to someone who assured me that he was Honey. Truthfully, I wished he were a cheeseburger.

One of the doctorologists came back in the room and chatted with Honey, who had mentioned that the last time we were in a hospital room together, we went home with a nearly ten-pound baby. But the happy juice still flowing in my veins had left me confused. I thought that the doctorologists were planning to present me with a postcolonoscopy gift of a new baby. Or did they say new puppy?

It's very hard to hear when you've just discovered you're wearing an adult diaper.

My Love God leaned in close and whispered that he'd seen my colonoscopy pictures while I was in la-la land. He felt that they were quite pretty, given they were taken from my least-flattering angle. I'm pretty sure he also said that he ordered double prints. In my groggy state, this near-compliment strangely pleased me. Then the bummologist popped in to tell me that the news was good. They didn't need to see me for another ten years!

Having a colonoscopy is not a bummer at all, but pro-crastination sure is.

So just grow up, show up, and say cheese.

PASSING THE TORCH

It was a beautiful summer day, so my Love God and I decided to take a drive through the North Carolina countryside. Surprisingly, we found ourselves talking about funerals, cremations, online bill paying, and finances—things that people often talk about as they get older so that they know their partners' thoughts and wishes.

My Love God has expressed a wish to be cremated, stored in a fishing tackle box, and then sprinkled on the salmon-fishing grounds off the coast of British Columbia in Canada. This is a long way from North Carolina, so the tackle-box urn and I would have to board a plane and hightail it to British Columbia after the service. I would keep the tackle-box urn stored safely in my tote bag under the airplane seat—I mean, what if I put him in the overhead bin and a careless passenger accidentally knocked his sprinkles out of the urn before we reached his final resting place with the salmon? One thing I know for sure is that my Love God does not wish to be scattered over row 22, seat D, on American Airlines Flight 1729.

As we were discussing these delicate topics, it hit me that I shouldn't get all of him cremated. Instead, I would like to keep his most valuable appendage close by to use it whenever I needed it. Honey agreed that this would be a good idea, and that I would need to ask the cremator person to carefully chop off the appendage after Honey passed. I think Honey was even touched by my desire to keep a part of him with me forever. We still haven't figured out how to keep the appendage stiff so that it works effectively after he passes, so this may be a problem. It's a wonderful thing when a husband and wife can talk about such matters, isn't it?

At this point, I feel that maybe I should back up a bit and explain how we came to this unusual decision. You see, when our talk involves Honey's passing on, it also involves talk of how bills will continue to get paid online, because Honey works that way. Much of that stuff eludes me, and—I'm being brutally honest here—I'm a fossil, as our youngest son says. I still even use a little black leather address book—just cross off the old address and phone number whenever the friend moves, and add the new information—I've done this for years. My little black book is like a little history book. Can't do that in a fancy little iPhone, now, can you?

So despite my desire to avoid technology talk in this life and the next, Honey told me for the umpteenth time that there were some things that I needed to be able to do in case he passed through the pearly gates unexpectedly—things like using his passwords, account numbers, websites, and all the stuff that the CFO of our house uses to keep track of our spending and piggy-bank balance. Now this is when I went into shock—Honey revealed that he uses his fingerprint to access certain financial accounts. *Oh great!* This may work well for him right now, but if he passes and is cremated, I am snookered.

This revelation then prompted us to discuss the best way to pass the financial torch to me, and that's when we decided it would be best if we just chopped off his finger after he passes, and then when it stiffened a little, I could use his fingerprint to access our accounts, just like he does. No switching fingerprints, passwords, and all that complicated stuff. Chop, chop—and then I could continue performing the CFO duties in our house without missing a beat.

You *did* think I meant his finger, didn't you?

FAT LIES

I had just announced to my Love God that I was going to join that famous weight-loss program for my second go-around. You know, the triumph of hope over experience. My lost weight had crept back, as it often does. So it was time to sign up again, pay my monthly dues, and waddle into the weekly meetings.

I went to my first meeting, version 2.0, and weighed in. I cringed as I saw my weight recorded in the record book. How did it get to this, I wondered? The last time I weighed myself, I weighed far less. Well, OK, that *was* two years ago. Time flies, and fat returns when you aren't paying attention.

With a straight face, my Love God then asked the forbidden question: "So what do you weigh?"—as if that were a normal marital question, like "Have you seen my sunglasses, dear?"

Did I hear that man correctly? Has he learned nothing after thirty years with me and fourteen with his first wife? OK, fine—if he insisted on asking a dumb question, I'd give him a dumb answer.

"I weigh one hundred fourteen pounds," I replied, looking him straight in the eye. That ought to stop him in his tracks. Let him prove I'm wrong. Silly man.

"One hundred fourteen—really?" he said, eyebrows raised. "That's very interesting."

I'd lied, and we both knew it. Let the games begin.

I wanted to dress as lightly as possible for my second weigh-in a week later, so I took my kitchen food scales into the bathroom to weigh various bras and panties. As I was leaving the bathroom, I was startled to meet my Love God in the doorway. He'd been watching me. I was like a deer caught in the headlights.

"What in heaven's name are you doing?" he asked.

I was tempted to lie again but braved the truth.

"I was weighing my underwear to see which pieces weighed the least."

He rolled his eyes and shook his head, trying to ignore this Lucy moment.

When I arrived home from the meeting, my Love God was waiting for me. "So how did the meeting go?" he asked. In Honey-speak that meant, "Did you lose any weight?"

"The meeting went well—I was down two and a half pounds."

"So what do you weigh now?"

Jeepers, did he think I was a mathematician? Lying is so complicated. I had to quickly recalculate my fake weight, subtracting 2.5 from 114 with him staring at me. My weigh-in record book told the truth, but this conversation was not about the truth.

This is the way it has gone for six months. Honey asks every week what my new weight is. I recalibrate my fake weight to correspond with my true weight loss. Apparently, I now weigh eighty-seven pounds, with a final weight goal of sixty-four pounds.

Oh, what a tangled web we weave…

NAVIGATING THE ROAD TO MARITAL BLISS

After driving nine hundred miles in a van loaded with three children and two dogs, my brother-in-law, Bryan, and sister-in-law, Joanne, were lost for more than two hours within ten miles of our house. I just couldn't understand how anyone using a GPS or MapQuest could get lost like that.

Then I learned the incredible truth: they had neither.

The long trip had apparently gone quite smoothly until they reached North Carolina. Joanne, the official navigator, had been buried under a blanket, happily watching a movie on her laptop for two hours, so by the time she surfaced from her movie tent, the snow-covered landscape was long gone, and they had zoomed right past the exit to Raleigh. Understandably, tension was running high in the love nest on wheels.

I'd like to suggest that it should be illegal for wives to navigate for their husbands. We never fold the map right, and we give directions like "turn now," which drives husbands insane. We also watch movies under tents when we should be following the map. There is no pleasing our husbands in matters involving navigation, so let's give it up to them. They can then both drive and navigate, which truthfully, they want to do anyway.

For our lost aliens, things just kept getting worse. Perplexed, Honey called Bryan and asked him why they didn't just follow the MapQuest route he had e-mailed to them. When Bryan sheepishly confessed that he had left the maps on the printer nine hundred miles back, I had to hold my Love God down in his chair.

Honey tried everything he could to help them by cell phone. He told them to look for Highway 98, which would get them to our house, but after twenty minutes, they called from the next county, unsure whether they were heading to California or the Atlantic Ocean. To warm up the icy atmosphere, Joanne was cheerfully pointing out all the beautiful Christmas lights, which brought screams from the rear car seat that this was the third time they had passed these houses. Even a fourth rerun of *Liar Liar* could not distract them. This was not *The Partridge Family* singing on the bus.

Despite more frantic phone calls, Honey could not figure out their location, so our daughter Jill and I jumped in the Suburban and headed east to escort them home if we ever found them. Through a series of calls relayed between the three phones like a Secret Service covert operation, we finally caught up with the wayward van and led the convoy home, arriving two hours past the original ETA.

Now for the obvious question: Other than the Griswolds, is there one family in the Western hemisphere that would undertake a nine-hundred-mile trip, through six populous states and an unfamiliar city, without a GPS or MapQuest? I asked my Love God this question, and he said that Bryan was, in fact, going to buy Joanne a GPS for Christmas, which was a great relief, as it would make their trip home less a nail-biter than the trip to us.

Christmas morning arrived. Joanne tore open a boxed gift, and suddenly a brand-new, lifesaving GPS appeared. Impressed and relieved, I asked Bryan where he'd bought it, and he said he'd bought it at a store near their home.

"*Whaaat*? You mean you had it in the van the entire nine hundred miles, and you never got it out to use it, even after you missed an exit and were lost for over two hours, with kids who were starving and dogs that had to pee?"

Looking like he hoped the floor would open so he could drop through it, Bryan said quietly, "But I wanted it to be a surprise."

Jeepers! It would have been a truly fabulous surprise if he had retrieved the GPS from the trunk as soon as they became lost. I'm sure that Santa would have understood the need for an emergency gift unwrapping, and he would certainly have kept the whole family on his "nice" list.

Here's all I know for sure: it took a strong and loving marriage to survive that trip without twenty-first-century navigational tools. If our marriage GPS ever breaks, I'm calling them for tips on how to navigate in tough times.

HAIR PEACE

For sixteen years I home-colored my hair, just as my mother had done before me. Why pay someone to wash away that gray when you could lock the bathroom door and come out forty minutes later looking like a refreshed version of yourself for just $6.39?

My hair horror began in my twenties when I started using Grecian Formula for men, but after a couple of years of daily dosing and smelling like men's aftershave, I yearned for a less-demanding hair solution.

The next step up the beauty ladder was to use semipermanent hair color, which had a weekly, not daily, routine. Every Saturday morning in my stained hair-coloring bathrobe, I would dye my hair. But the problem with this semipermanent dye was that the color faded with each daily shampoo, so by Friday I had washed my way through seven different hair shades. My friends could tell what day of

the week it was just by the shade of my hair: *There's Diane...*
oh, it must be Wednesday.

Not looking the same two days in a row became ex-
tremely stressful, so I decided I would upgrade to a *perma-*
nent hair color in a shade coincidentally called Diana. Every
third or fourth Saturday morning, I'd casually emerge
from the bathroom, pretending that I'd been flossing my
teeth for forty minutes. I always kept two or three boxes of
Diana on hand, even taking a box on a vacation to Greece
so I wouldn't be caught with gray hair.

Those were my various hair routines for sixteen years,
over a two-husband period. My first husband, Mr. Wrong,
once remarked that my freshly dyed hair looked like a
helmet; our divorce was final about three months later.
However, my Love God, an earlier graduate of husband
school, always refrained from unsolicited hair reviews, and
thus we've been happily married for many years.

By age forty-five, I was tired of this unrelenting hair
routine and asked my Love God for his forthright opinion
on letting my hair go gray. He ducked the loaded question, saying, "Do whatever you want, dear," so I decided
that I *would* do what I wanted, and what I wanted was to
stop coloring my hair. Gray roots were too demanding; I
decided that I hated the coloring routine more than I hated
the thought of having gray hair. I had colored my hair for
the last time.

Fired up by my bravado, I announced to the all-male
management team at my office that I was letting my hair
go gray and that if anyone said one word, he would be

deleted from the payroll system. I vividly recall them sitting through my gray hair rant, mindlessly picking donut sprinkles out of their teeth.

My hair color had become a brown, brassy orange and white mixture, much like tiger-tail ice cream—a good thing in a waffle cone but pathetic-looking on my head. But I held my tricolored head high as I counted the weeks until my next haircut, which would remove another inch of "tress mess." I avoided looking in mirrors.

When I was with my husband in the car and he couldn't escape, I would voice my anxieties about going gray, second-guessing my decision daily. At his wit's end, he said he didn't want to hear about my hair color ever again. Translating his man-speak, that meant *color it or don't color it—just be happy with yourself.* Finally, we had agreed on something: I just wanted to be happy with myself too.

The tipping point in my gray hair reinvention came ten months into my journey. As I boarded a plane to New York, the flight attendant said she loved my hair. I looked around, wondering to whom she was talking, but I was the only one there. Over the next three days, two more people said they loved my hair. Did my Love God pay off these big-city people with promises of his famous barbequed ribs if they would speak kindly about my hair? This trip was an omen to me, a sign from the hair gods. My gray hair would stay.

It took eighteen long months to grow out my tiger-tail hair. I no longer feared that my gray roots would creep in, revealing me as a fake. I decided that if someone wasn't going to like the real me because I had gray hair or wrinkles or a muffin top, then we never had a shot at friendship anyway.

My husband was my true compass during my year-and-a-half reinvention. I have always been thankful that I chose a partner for whom it was never all about my hair or my looks. He said it was my personality, intelligence, and smile that won him over. I was overwhelmed by his support and maturity.

So what will be my personal beauty philosophy as I get older? To strive for an A in physical perfection would require me to think about myself too much, which is boring to me and certainly to others. I'd become a woman consumed by my shortfalls, by my physical imperfections—a glass half empty, not half full. Instead, I want to wear my age with grace, confidence, and contentedness. I expect there will be many Cs but also, I hope, a couple of As and Bs for character, humor, and personality.

No longer under the spell of hair color, I can see that the fountain of youth for any woman is this: a heartfelt smile, a sense of humor, and a sincere interest in other people. Our physical attributes cannot outrun the passage of time. But no woman at any age can look unattractive or old if she is laughing, smiling, or engaged with others.

As I ponder gray hair and other facts of aging, this is what I have come to think:

Gray can be great. Gray hair is best for secure women with nongray personalities who have confidence, self-esteem, and chutzpah.

Know your true value. Reinvent yourself using *all your talents*, beyond your looks. Talent, creativity, and character hold their value longer than a youthful facade. Don't get trapped in your high-school-prom-queen image in which your looks were your currency. The prom is so over.

Keep your redo list short. If you find that you have a *very* long redo list, there's a chance that the real issue may not be your looks at all. Sorry...I'm just saying.

After I said good riddance to Diana hair color, I would babble clichés like *it's less expensive* or *it's easier this way*, but none of these excuses was the truth. The truth was that I became very comfortable with gray hair, being different and daring to stand apart from the crowd. No more whining, no more apologies, and no more excuses.

My hair and I are at finally at peace.

MY BATHING-SUIT GIRDLE

It's a sunny morning on the lake, and we're cruising in our boat called *Jeepers*, which is also my Love God's favorite expletive. I'm perched on the back seat of the boat wearing Jackie O sunglasses and a black spandex bathing suit that I'm hoping will serve effectively as a girdle too.

I don't take wearing a bathing suit lightly—I chopped down the hair on my legs and underarms before coming to the boat, but lacking time and motivation, I left my "bikini line" untouched. It's a tricky area to maneuver around, mainly because my line of sight is obstructed by my stomach, which leaves everything in my southern hemisphere a mystery to me. I would need four-foot-long arms and a series of mirrors arranged just so to give me a perfect view of the "line." It might as well be the Mason-Dixon Line because I've never seen that either, and I've been on serious watch for both since moving to the Land of Y'all.

I'm enjoying the boat ride until I see a sign on the boat that says the maximum capacity is seven persons and 1,050 pounds. With nothing much else for my brain to chew on, I worry that the coast guard will stop us on our cruise and demand that we get weighed on a big fish scale. I quickly do the math. There are five people in the boat, so we are safe on the people count, but if we average 210 pounds or more, we're in serious trouble. I start to panic. We're clearly a hefty bunch, so my worry is justified. Will we be fined by the pound? Do we have to throw one person overboard to meet this strict requirement? Will the lake police blame me because I had two extra pancakes for breakfast?

Mrs. Pascoe, it's your fault the boat sank because you wolfed down those pancakes that you had no business eating. Can't you see the strain on the seams of your bathing-suit girdle?

I come out of my daydream with a start, happy to see the boat still floating and the coast guard nowhere in sight.

"Pass the water and carrots, please." There is nothing like the threat of getting on the scales in front of six people to help a woman focus.

CONFESSIONS OF A CONTEST ADDICT

I love contests. Coloring contests, writing contests, prom queen contests, and contests of skill or luck—I've entered them all. Heck, I'd eat thirteen Big Macs in thirteen minutes if it meant I could win the title of Miss Golden Arches.

Although I mostly lose these contests, on the rarest of occasions, I win. You know, the triumph of hope over experience and skill.

In grade two I was in a square-dancing contest but twirled too much, got separated from my partner, and ended up in last place. I never square danced again.

Then in grade five, I misspelled the word "vacuum" in a spelling bee and was eliminated. For the record, I still feel it's wrong that a word has two *u*'s smack beside each other. But I'm no longer bitter. Really, I'm not.

Ever hopeful of being named the winner of something—*anything*—I recently entered an online "beauty" contest sponsored by my favorite women's magazine. Before you laugh, I'm well aware that I'm not a beauty by any standard. But there are a few people, perhaps with a special type of Tourette's, who periodically have blurted out compliments despite some overwhelming objective evidence to the contrary. Nevertheless, I thought I'd enter this contest to try to win two bus tickets to New York for my Love God and me. We could even pack some sandwiches and a few bags of Cheetos for the bus trip so we could save our money for fun in the Big Apple. I was starting to get excited.

Until yesterday, that is, when I checked the contest scoreboard and was shocked to see that one contestant had more than eight thousand votes with a month left to go. I had to work hard to muster up forty-four votes by e-mailing all my kind friends, who, despite thinking I was nuts and not beautiful, vowed to click on my photo to help me win the bus trip I coveted. Even my friend Sandra, who took it upon herself to lead a campaign to get votes for me, threw in the towel after only two days when she saw the gap in the score. To get more votes than the leading lady, I'd need a daily "yes" click from every person I had ever met since kindergarten. Won't happen.

By now, many women were trouncing me in votes— not just the leading lady. My Love God, who can always pick the beauty-pageant winners on TV, offered his wise opinion once he studied the entrants carefully.

"The reason they have way more votes than you, Di, is that they have run marathons and you haven't."

Whoa, I didn't see that coming.

"But I walked in the four-mile Furry Scurry with the dogs and even in the eight-kilometer Turkey Trot last year," I protested. "Maybe it's not too late—there's still a month left, you know. Maybe there's a marathon I can walk in somewhere in this state."

Honey shook his head. "Diane, people *run* in marathons. They don't *walk*. And not only that, you didn't write about those walks in your contest entry story, and you can't make changes to your story once you submit it. So, quite frankly, you're toast."

Those are harsh words for an incurable contest addict to hear. I optimistically thought that a photo of me with no sesame seeds in my teeth and an amusing little story about my hot-coral-lipstick obsession would put me on the podium. I never even considered the need to put fitness achievements in my application. Or maybe I was just a bit *too* honest about my wrinkles. Or maybe I should've spray-painted my gray hair a golden blond before Honey snapped my photo. Or maybe I could have volunteered at the hospital or joined the Peace Corps to be a better person.

Shoulda, woulda, coulda. It was too late to worry about the contest. I'd had my chance. I only hoped I didn't come in dead last. At least I managed to get thirteen unsolicited votes from total strangers *before* I started twisting my friends' arms to click on my photo out of loyalty or perhaps out of pity.

But with each contest I enter, I learn some valuable lessons:

- It's good to put ourselves out there to achieve anything in life, so let's all get going.
- Practice spelling "vacuum" and maybe even "aardwolf" in case they come up in a spelling bee.
- Don't twirl too much in life. It makes you dizzy and confused.
- If I'm going to enter a marathon, I first need to learn to run.
- I will try writing seriously occasionally. It's good practice for contests.
- Assuming I won't ever write seriously, I'll only enter humor-writing contests.

Most importantly, I should enter contests that I have some chance of winning—contests that are specifically for women with gray hair and red lips, who prefer to walk rather than run, who have a fabulous marriage, great kids, and a charmed life, even with its challenges.

Oh wait, I've already won that contest!

NOISES IN THE NIGHT

Carley, our dachshund, is frightened of many things. She hides under the bed when there's lightning and thunder. She runs the other way when car mufflers backfire. July 4 is a nightmare for her, not a celebration, because fireworks explode loudly in the sky. She even barks at the ice maker when it's making ice. But this list is not exhaustive—we have just added one more fear.

Carley is afraid of farts—her own, to be specific.

I learned of her newest fear last night for the first time. Out of nowhere she jumped on the bed and bounced onto my pillow, kissing and licking me, then lying across my neck like a dachshund neck warmer. This was an impossible sleeping arrangement for me—I couldn't breathe, let alone sleep. She seemed anxious and afraid. Did she have a doggie nightmare where she was being chased by a squirrel? Worried, I woke up Honey, who suggested that she had slept all day and mustn't be tired. Nah, she always sleeps all day but never behaves like this.

Suddenly Carley bounced across the blanket to seek comfort from Honey. As she bounced, I heard two loud *pffft* sounds from her rear quarter. You can call them any indelicate term you like—booty belches, putt putts, duck calls, butt burps, pop tarts, puffers—we all know what I'm talking about. Scared by these noises, the wiener girl took cover by lying on Honey's chest with her head on his shoulder. She wouldn't budge.

"Honey, did you just hear Carley toot?" I asked. I had never actually heard her puff out loud in all the years we've had her. I think she is normally the silent-but-deadly type, where you must cover your nose while you wonder which dog or person cut the cheese. Tonight it was different— she made loud noises.

"I sure did hear that. Did she eat something weird today?"

Hmmm—let me think back through her meals. I think it was a normal food day for the wiener girl. Let me see now...she ate dog kibble, granola cereal and milk, chewy chicken strips, Milk-Bones, a cheddar cheese slice, carrots, a bit of ham, and maybe some Cheetos—nothing unusual, really. Well, OK—I do recall that she might have had a meatball or two with chili grape sauce. And now that I'm thinking about it, I believe Carley had her first taste of coleslaw with bits of pomegranate and pineapple—good, healthy fiber foods on the food pyramid, right?

Maybe not—coleslaw is mostly cabbage, a well-known toot producer. The meatballs had some seasonings too, which may have caused a tempest in her tummy. And not to get too personal, but even Honey was a bit noisy himself last night—like father, like daughter, maybe?

OK, starting tomorrow, we will try to limit her to kibble, Milk-Bones, and carrots. And just to be safe, in case we weaken, I'm going to buy her some doggie earmuffs so she doesn't scare herself with her putt putts.

HOW MY HUSBAND GAVE ME A FACELIFT

Family photos of me fall into one of three unattractive categories: I am either wearing my sunglasses like Roy Orbison in drag, sleeping with my mouth wide open, or looking stunned when surprised by my Love God jumping out from behind the fake ficus tree. The family, of course, enjoys these pictures very much.

So it's become quite clear that I need a more flattering picture that *resembles* me but looks *a bit better* than me. I tell Honey we are on a mission, and there's no time to waste. I ask him to crank up the camera while I slap on some lipstick, trying hard to stay inside the lines, and then run a near-toothless comb through my 226 hairs. I decide to go all out, adding some cover-up makeup and a swash of plum blush, which leaves my right cheek looking a bit bruised. I'm hoping it will fade with the camera flash.

I plop down on the kitchen stool. My photographer/ Love God starts clicking madly. He asks me to sit still, or my pictures will be fuzzy, which I secretly think would be a good thing. He turns the lights off and then turns them back on, adjusting every dial on the camera, while I check my teeth for lipstick smears. I try to sit up straight so I don't look like the Hunchback of Notre Dame, but it's putting a kink in my neck.

Honey keeps clicking and then checks the results on the camera screen. Looking over his shoulder, I can see a lamp protruding out of one ear and a doorknob out of the other. *Jeepers, he could have checked the background behind me before he started clicking!*

I smile every which way I know, but I'm out of practice due to the fact I've usually been near unconscious when my pictures have been taken. Why didn't I take a few extra minutes to practice my smile in the mirror? Too late now. Honey declares the session is over—a wrap. We head to the computer where he uploads the pictures so we can have a good laugh...I mean a good look.

OMG! My forehead is so furrowed that I could plant soy beans in the grooves. And since when did my fingers resemble sausages with nails? You'd better get ready to hit the delete button, Honey—these pictures must never see the light of day.

Where did all these chins and smile creases come from? I normally don't see these flaws because I suspect I look in the mirror holding my head just so, staring straight ahead but with a slight upturn of my chins to stretch my neck out a bit. I usually squint while looking at the pictures to improve my image, but I can't expect others to follow my squinting instructions just to see me in the best possible light.

I suggest to my photographer/Love God that he try the computer's *erase* feature on one or more of my chins, so he drags the eraser over my second chin. Bam! The extra chin disappears…but wait a minute! Now my head merges right into my neck so that I look like a peg head. I beg Honey to reverse these deformities, but he can't find the Undo button! I will be resigned to a life in the family photo album as the no-neck woman if he can't fix this. I'm starting to panic.

Honey moves quickly to the next picture, where he does all the lighting adjustments, and then he hits the rejuvenation jackpot. The Remove Noise button magically softens thirty years of creases, wrinkles, and splotches. *Now we're getting somewhere!* The electronic Botox is finally working.

But wait a minute! Now I'm starting to look *too* good. Nobody will ever believe it's me. Even *I* don't believe it's me. Bam! Honey moves the pointer halfway back so I look more like me—minus a year or five. Some wrinkles are back, and my virtual facelift is complete.

At long last I have some pictures of me conscious, dressed, made up, and not looking like Roy Orbison.

MY ONE AND ONLY SUCCESSFUL
NEW YEAR'S RESOLUTION

Changing a habit is tough, as anyone who has ever tried knows. And New Year's is that time when we resolve to be the person we dream of being. A New Year's resolution is typically our first big lie of the year.

Over the years I've made resolutions about losing weight, saving more money, spending less money, not biting my nails, seeing my friends more, seeing miserable people less, and any other behaviors I felt I needed to change to become a better human being. New Year's resolutions have rarely worked because my motivation didn't come from within, but, instead, from that date on the calendar. I'd lose my focus and lose my way, just in time for chocolate truffles on February 14.

Then one Christmas I attended a women's luncheon where we were asked to write down one goal or resolution that we wanted to achieve the following year. The resolution lady said we should share our resolution with the nine other women at the table and then write it on a piece of paper that would go inside a self-addressed envelope. The following December, our resolutions would be mailed to us at home.

It then started to dawn on me what was happening. That resolution lady was trying to make me *accountable to myself* for achieving my resolution. I had never written down a resolution before because it made it so...so *serious*. I think I preferred treating a resolution more as a dream than as a goal, so then I didn't have to give up or to start any new behaviors that I really didn't want to. Twisted thinking, I realize, but this is exactly why habits usually undermine resolutions.

I decided that if I were going to go along with this activity, then my resolution had to be important to me, different from my usual well-worn resolutions, to have a fair chance of success. My resolution-by-mail met all these criteria: I was going to learn to play golf. I had my career and my family, but I had no hobby or activity that qualified as fun, except maybe having a pedicure once a month. It was also hard to join golf events at work without completely embarrassing myself. I swing a golf club like a baseball bat, I've been told on more than one occasion.

I sealed the envelope and handed it in nervously. I'd worry all year long about that envelope arriving in the mail in December. I was not going to say a word to my Love God until spring, for fear he would have me out on the golf course on the first snowfall, wearing webbed snow-shoes in two feet of white stuff, whacking hot-pink golf balls. Honey is not a procrastinator.

As I drove by the local golf course one spring day, it struck me that my resolution deadline was creeping closer, so I finally shared my resolution with Honey, knowing I'd need his golf advice if I ever expected to have a score under three hundred. As a further incentive, I bought a golf wardrobe for my new hobby. There was nothing like a new pair of two-toned shoes to motivate me, even if they did have metal cleats.

I really enjoyed playing golf that summer, which was, of course, the whole point of having a hobby in the first place. And when the mailman arrived in December with my envelope, I felt great satisfaction at having fulfilled my commitment to myself. I think they call it pride, but I considered it my first hole in one.

Though I am hardly a pro golfer, I have added a new dimension to my life by learning to play golf. More importantly, I learned a few things about resolutions:

- Never lose sight of why life will be better when you achieve your resolution. If you ever lose sight of this, you will make the wrong choice when challenged.
- Fight the temptation to sabotage yourself by making excuses that would earn you a Pulitzer Prize for fiction. Tell others about your goal so that they

can support you and help you keep the faith. They want you to succeed too.

- Making a personal resolution is really the same process as setting goals at work: write them down, discuss them with your team, and follow up regularly to see if you're on track. This is probably why that famous weight-loss program works, when so many other approaches fail.

Perhaps this New Year's is the right time to make a resolution about a new way of making resolutions, particularly if your old approaches haven't worked. This could be the first New Year's when your resolution is a hole in one for you too.

DREAM A LITTLE DREAM

My dream started off as a little family joke, as dreams often do. It's not like I was dreaming big, hoping to cure cancer or make Congress agree on something, but I'd set a goal for myself where the odds of achieving it seemed very much against me. I'm talking about getting my picture on the jumbotron at an NHL hockey game.

I've been going to NHL hockey games for many years, occasionally in Nashville or Atlanta but mostly in Raleigh, and at every game I see cameramen filming painted faces, cute blond girls, and people with homemade signs. They even film couples snuggling and little boys with facial contortions so bizarre that you pray their faces won't get stuck like that.

But most often, the cameramen just sneak up on people who are staring blankly into space, while their seatmates furiously elbow them to look up at the jumbo-tron. To be clear, I don't stare into space, mainly because I'm too busy smiling at the cameraman, hoping to attract his attention. I'm always on high alert, eager to see my mug on the screen for a split second. OK, maybe for five seconds.

Not to be too boastful, but I've come close to being a "jumbo star" a couple of times. One time the camera was zooming in on my lime-green sweater, but it suddenly veered to the right, focusing on the young blonde beside me. Only my green sleeve made the big screen. Fast-forward to last year when a cameraman took shots of my stomach and kneecaps while filming the exotic beauty in the seat directly in front of me. Of course, nobody knew they were *my* body parts, so it didn't count toward achieving my dream. And my dream has been fading fast, given that my Love God and I usually sit in the *value section* (OK, the cheap seats) on the third level, where the cameramen rarely venture, except if there's a drunken fan dancing the Macarena or the Chicken Dance.

But last night was different. We were sitting in seats close to the ice, a gift from less-frugal friends. As always, I was looking eagerly at the cameraman, who, having just made eye contact with me, raised his camera and pointed it in my direction. I was hopeful but wary—there was probably a Playboy bunny lurking behind me or a child with his tongue stuck out somewhere in my vicinity. Or perhaps he mistook me for Doris Day. Some friends say I resemble her, except for my hair, figure, face, clothes, and singing voice. Must be we have similar feet. Or maybe he noticed that I was looking unusually well-groomed for a hockey fan, having just had my hair cut and coiffed.

Whatever the reason the camera lingered…and then it happened.

"Look, you're on the jumbotron!" Honey said. Oh my gosh, there I was with my 1980s hot coral lipstick and freshly cut mane. Oh sure, there were seven or eight other people in the picture, including Honey. But frankly, I had eyes only for me, as I grinned and waved furiously at the camera. I'd finally achieved my jumbotron dream without even having to leap around in my cow costume or carry a sign declaring my undying love for the hockey player who was my current favorite.

As if my jumbotron jubilation weren't enough, I even received e-mails from two attentive friends saying they saw me on TV, which transported me briefly from a faceless hockey fan to a TV starlet.

Dreams do come true; they can happen to you. The song got it so right.

In the overall scheme of things, I know that getting on the jumbotron at a hockey game doesn't matter a hill of beans. I also know that I happened to be in the right place at the right time, and probably most important, I was wearing the right lipstick. But isn't that when dreams come true—when you show up, when you are trying your best, and when you give it your all and don't give up, even when the odds are against you?

Here's what I know for sure: it isn't the size of the dream that's important but having a dream at all. Dreams give life possibilities, and possibilities give life purpose.

SLEEPING OUT LOUD

"What's bothering you, dear?"

Honey's question pierced the early-morning stillness. The only other sound was the dog's elbow thumping the floor while giving his ears their morning scratch.

"Oh, I'm just thinking about all the things that have to be done," I explained sleepily. As an afterthought I asked curiously, "How did you know I was awake?"

A pause followed; then he said, "Because you were so quiet."

Hmmm.

Flashback to one night about three years earlier. As I lay peacefully in my presleep frozen-ferret position, Honey walked over to my side of the bed and bent down with his nose to my face. I waited for a good-night kiss, but there was no smooch.

In the morning I asked him what that was all about, and he replied, "You were sleeping more quietly than usual, so I came close to see if you were dead."

Call me dense, but it was only at that moment that I realized he was just too gentlemanly to tell me I snore, or "sleep out loud," as Mark Twain once put it. Questions raced through my mind. Would I score a ten on the snoring Richter scale? Did I exceed the safety limits for noise? I knew better than to challenge his observation because he could record me at my symphonic worst, ending all hope that maybe he was just teasing me, as spouses often do. Deep down, though, I knew it was true because I've even snorted *myself* awake, hearing just the tail end of a freight train leaving my pillow as I awoke.

I worry a lot about snoring. What if I fall asleep on an airplane, and there is no Honey there to nudge me? Will the flight attendant ask me to turn it down a notch or two because the other passengers can't hear *Mrs. Doubtfire Returns?* Will everyone stare at me as I play my nasal trumpet in dreamland?

Horrors! I must never fall asleep in a public place, I vow to myself.

This vow, however, was very short lived. My friend Violette and I recently fell asleep at the beach in the relaxing, warm sun, snorting ourselves awake after a few minutes of sawing logs and drooling. At my snoring worst, Honey says I could cause a tsunami, wiping out all beach life on the East Coast.

When those ads appear on TV for the pills, gizmos, and gadgets that guarantee snore-free sleep, my Love God turns his head ever so slightly toward me, with his eyebrows raised, silent. He learned in husband school that silence saves marriages.

My Love God is lovingly tolerant of my nasal noise, putting a positive spin on this annoyance. "I just think of it as your mating call," he explains.

This is proof to me that love is not only blind—it's deaf too.

TINKLE, TINKLE, I'M A STAR

I'm pretty sure there's not a writer alive who doesn't enjoy at least a teeny bit of recognition for that special way they string words together. So you can imagine how flattered I was when an article appeared in our company newsletter about my humor essays, which were featured in an online women's magazine. This revelation created a brief flurry of excitement in the office halls with my coworkers, who seemed genuinely surprised that I could write something other than e-mails or warning letters for wayward employees.

So you can imagine my surprise one evening when I was walking down the back stairwell at work and a woman's voice called out, "Hi, there—are you that writer?"

Good heavens! I turned around to look at my new fan, and there was the office cleaning lady leaning on her broom, smiling at me. Well, I'll be doggone. I guess that picture of me in the company newsletter did me justice.

"Miss Diane, could you print me some of those stories you've written? I'd like to read them on my breaks and when I go to the bathroom."

The bathroom reading part struck me as curious, but I eagerly responded. "Sure. I hope you enjoy them—thanks for asking!" I scurried back to my office to print the stories and then rushed them over to her. The way I see it, you never know when you'll get another fan, so you'd better work hard to keep the few you have. I left the building smiling at my stairwell fame.

A few days later, the cleaning lady approached me again, asking for another set of my essays for her sister to read when she went to the bathroom. I was dumbfounded. Scribbling a collection of essays for bathroom reading was hardly on my publishing bucket list. To be honest, I had been dreaming about a charming little humor book that would be on every woman's nightstand, not on her toilet tank.

My dream went like this: A big-city literary agent would read my essays online one afternoon while she enjoyed a crispy chicken sandwich at McYummy's. Her jaw would drop in amazement as she read the witty part. She would run out of the restaurant to catch the last JetBlue flight to Raleigh, eager to meet me before I had tucked in for the night. She would bang on the front door, flashing a book contract in my sleepy face, delighting me with promises of publishing my ditties in forty-two languages, including

Tasmanian. I'd breathlessly sign the contract while smiling for pictures to promote my book tour across seven continents. My delightful little book would rival *Gone with the Wind* and even *The Cat in the Hat*.

One thing I absolutely knew for certain: I was not put on this earth to write a bathroom reader for *tinklers*. Or was I? Maybe the cleaning lady was onto something. My mind started to race. Is it possible my precious essays could serve a higher purpose in the bathrooms of the nation? Could my shorter ditties encourage little tinkles and the longer ones be an amusing distraction when bowel business was, uuhhh, slow? Heck, women could even learn a bit about lipstick, weight loss, or even marital bliss with Honey, often topics of interest for the modern madam.

Maybe I could get my life chronicles published on the doors of women's bathroom stalls. I could even have home parties where I could sell my bathroom books or have them available through iTunes so they could be downloaded for easy bathroom listening.

I could see the letterhead of my new company: *Ms. Pascoe's Bathroom Omni Media*, much like Martha Stewart's empire but with a lavatory theme. I could have velour hand towels and washcloths with my image adorning them and perhaps toilet paper decorated with some of my more endearing quips. Stephanie, a fabulous online magazine editor, would be interviewed for the foreword and would say she knew me before I became a famous bathroom-reader writer, and yes, she too was surprised that I'd chosen this genre.

Warming up to my new calling as a bathroom-reader writer, I even started to dream up titles for this tome of toilet prose, like *Tinkle, Tinkle, I'm a Star* or *Tales from the Throne*. I could envision my words in bathrooms all over the world.

Move over, Erma. It's my turn now.

PILLOW TALK

It started out simply enough. I needed to buy a new pillow.

One night, my Love God whispered that his pillow was a bit flat and that he needed a new pillow to keep his neck from straining when he slept. Eager to please and with no paying job, I put his request on the top of my non-existent priority list and set out the next morning for the department store.

It's a funny thing about pillows—you buy them when you marry but never think to replace them, no matter how squished and discolored they get. I'm psyched up for this pillow challenge and stride through the store aisles confidently. I spy stacks of puffy, fluffy, clean pillows in plastic bags. Perfect!

I study the slumber selection—standard, queen, king, European, quilted, firm, foam, fluffy, and feathers in every configuration possible. I'm starting to feel a little dizzy, as the choice for the perfect pillow for my Love God is not obvious. Why wasn't my Love God more specific about the pillow technology he wanted when he made his request? What if I buy one that is too firm and he gets a stiff neck or becomes disabled? What if it is too soft and he smothers—death by down?

Sweat is starting to form on my nose as I contemplate the gravity of my decision. Frustrated and fed up, I make up my mind to just buy them all. I make my way to the cashier with nine billowy pillows clutched under my arms and in my sweaty hands.

I reach the cashier and throw my feathery flock onto the belt. The sweat drips onto the pillows as I grope for my wallet. Another customer approaches from behind, eyeing my pile of fluff.

"Are pillows on sale?" she asks innocently.

Jeepers, doesn't she know about neck safety, personal comfort, and the like? It's not about a pillow sale, dearie; it's about my buying the right pillow for Honey, for heaven's sake.

Now, did I remember to get a contoured orthopedic pillow? Maybe that will do the trick. Darn it! It's too late—the cashier is ringing in my mountains of foam and fowl.

"That will be one hundred seventeen dollars and twenty-three cents," says the cashier. "How would you like to pay?"

Yikes! How could I come to the store to buy one new pillow but end up buying nine pillows costing $117.23? How will I explain this to the family when I'm sent to debtor's prison, where the pillows are unquestionably terrible? I hand her my never-been-used new debit card. She swipes it through the machine.

"Please input your PIN, ma'am."

Merry Christmas! I have no idea what my PIN is. Is it E-R-I-C or C-I-R-E? 1-2-3-4 or 4-3-2-1? What secret code did I select, hoping I'd never forget it? So many cards, so many PINs, so many pillows. I know I wrote that code down somewhere, but with the customer line behind me getting long, I must forget using the debit card. I hand the cashier my no-code-needed VISA card. I'll just sign on the line and get the heck out of pillow purgatory.

"Have a nice day," says the cashier.

Easy for her to say. She didn't have to buy a pillow.

MY LOVE GOD'S EX-WIFE'S BROCCOLI SALAD

Before anyone gets all worked up thinking that this is an ugly story about my husband and his ex-wife, I can assure you it isn't. In fact, he's always said that she was smart, an excellent cook, and very pretty, but like thousands of marriages, including my own to Mr. Wrong, it didn't work out.

But my stepwife and my Love God husband have maintained pleasant relations because they really love their children, and he really loves her recipes. Many years ago she was generous enough to write out some favorite recipes for him, likely having heard his teary tale that I could use some guidance in the kitchen. That is how her broccoli-salad recipe became a favorite in our home. I'm planning to prepare it for a cookout tomorrow, so I need to go to the Food Tiger to buy the ingredients.

I'm off to a great start. The broccoli is right where I expect it to be in the produce section, so I grab three bundles and then scurry up and down the aisles, hunting for the sliced water chestnuts. Water chestnuts are a vegetable, right? Or are they a nut, as in chestnut? I check the canned vegetables and the nut sections but come up empty. *Notice that I'm still in a good mood.*

Now let me think—where would the sunflower seeds and raisins be? I'll bet they're in the nuts or baking products sections. I waddle up and down a few aisles, but alas, no raisins or sunflower seeds. *My stepwife's broccoli salad is starting to get on my nerves.*

For the record, I've shopped for these salad fixings quite successfully at least one hundred times in the past thirty years. Maybe my inability to find the water chestnuts is a sign of old-timer's disease. Maybe I'm ready for the home for the forgetful. Maybe they even have a double room for Honey and me, who has been calling me Debbie lately.

Without these last three ingredients, my stepwife's recipe will not be very tasty. I might as well just serve a plate of broccoli flowerets with French onion dip. But I'm not a quitter, no way. I've even scored 100 percent on the "goal focus" factor on those personality tests that employers make you take to see what's wrong with you.

Finally, I catch a glimpse of a man in a white coat near the chicken wings. He is either a store employee or a man from the home who has been called to come and get me. I ask Mr. White Coat Man if he knows where the sunflower seeds are. He says he has no idea (see, it's not just *me*), but he uses his headset to call for help; then he says, "They're above the beef jerky in aisle five." This is news to me.

I test him again, this time asking him where the water chestnuts are. He heads to the Asian section with me in hot pursuit. Nestled between the bamboo shoots and rice wafers are the sliced water chestnuts. I grab two cans like they're Olympic trophies.

I have one final question for my white-coat escort: "Can you tell me where I can find raisins? I just can't seem to find them in the usual places."

"No problem," he says, looking quite pleased with his record of accomplishment so far. He dashes to aisle four to show me the raisins hiding between the brown gravy mixes and the fruit cocktail cans. Who knew?

With all the ingredients for my stepwife's broccoli salad in hand, I head to the cash register so I can get home before the broccoli is completely wilted. A young missy at the checkout asks me if I found everything I was looking for. *Nope, not going there, missy. You do not have enough time today to hear my tale of woe.*

By the way, my Love God's ex-wife's broccoli salad was fabulous, as always. Kudos once again to my stepwife, but after today's experience, I'm going to pass her broccoli recipe over to the chef at the home for the forgetful, where Honey and I will be moving—much sooner than we had planned, I suspect. I will let someone else worry about finding the ingredients for my stepwife's fabulous broccoli salad.

MY LOVE GOD'S EX-WIFE'S BROCCOLI-SALAD RECIPE

2 large heads of broccoli, chopped into small florets
1 cup chopped celery
1 cup chopped green onions (or as desired)
1 can sliced water chestnuts
1 cup raisins (can use dried cranberries)
1 cup unsalted, shelled sunflower seeds
1/2 lb. bacon (fried and crumbled)

Dressing: add just before serving
1 cup mayonnaise
2 tbsp. lemon juice
1–2 tsp. sugar (or as you desire)

SHOULD YOUR LIPSTICK MATCH YOUR CELL PHONE?

I know many people think I have an obsessive-compulsive disorder, but I don't think I do. I just love buying lipstick. Well, OK, I do admit that I have toyed with the idea of lipstick psychotherapy, but if I spent money on that, I would have nothing left for more lipsticks, would I? I'm experiencing the classic catch-22 of the fashion-conscious but financially depleted woman.

With such a passion for lip color, and with tubes galore in my bathroom drawer, you can imagine my joy at realizing that my phone case was exactly the color I was looking for in a new lipstick. So here's my new lipstick-hunting technique—I hold my phone up as I walk through the cosmetics department like I'm expecting a winning call from the state lottery, but all the while I'm using the phone case to make a match with the lipsticks in the counter displays. It's a brilliant concept, really.

One day while I was using my lipstick-hunting method in the cosmetic aisles at Macy's, I spotted a flash of hot coral at the lipstick counter the next aisle over. Now here's the curious thing—I can't see crumbs on the kitchen counter or spider webs in the corner, but I sure can pick out a new lipstick shade at fifty feet. It's just a special talent I possess.

As I approached the counter, a store clerk with blond hair-sprayed hair sweetly asked me if I was looking for a lipstick.

Yes, of course a lipstick, I thought snidely. Did she think I was looking for a roasted chicken? I'll confess I'm a tad sensitive about my lipstick fixation.

"Well, doesn't that bright-red lipstick look just beautiful with your tan," the sales lady exclaimed.

Wanting to believe she was right, I smiled and thanked her. But I've heard salesclerks say kind things to customers that eavesdroppers like me know are just not true, so I must discount her compliment, regrettably. I've experienced retail flattery like this in the past, such as the following:

- "What a lovely color your hair is!" (Translation: gray is not much of a color.)
- "Your lipstick is so beautiful and bright. I've never seen that color before." (Translation: that color belongs on a baboon's butt.)

But despite my skepticism, I tried to take her almost-compliment in the right spirit because it was Christmas, after all, and 'twas the season to be jolly.

The salesclerk continued, "Your tan looks lovely—is it fake or real?" Whoa! She might as well have asked me my bra size, for heaven's sake. Can't a woman keep her beauty secrets a secret anymore? What gives a woman with blond hair-sprayed hair the right to expose my phoniness?

"It's fake," I mumbled. Feeling a tad defensive, I continued, "I really just use a teeny, tiny bit of tanner occasionally to make sure my hair and skin don't match." Exactly why I was explaining all this to a woman I had just met, I have no idea!

"Well, for a fake tan, it looks fairly real," the woman said. "What kind of tanner do you use? You know, you must be careful because it can creep into your wrinkles and forehead lines, making them look like furrows in a field. But, of course, *your* skin doesn't look all that bad."

It was sounding worse the more she talked. I'd sunk from "beautiful" to "lovely" to "not all that bad." Then came the punch line: "How about we do a makeover on you?"

Wait one little moment, missy. What happened to "beautiful"? What about my fabulous lipstick color? Why do you want to erase this special-if-not-outdated look and redo it in something close to this year's style? Hundreds of clerks before you have chased me down the cosmetic aisles hoping to correct what nature and I have worked hard to mess up, and I have outrun them all.

"Good heavens!" I whispered to the blond salesclerk, "It would take you three or four hours to fix this face—no time today! No, ma'am—I don't want you to use up your precious time just to turn me into a *Thoroughly Modern Millie* that nobody will recognize. What if friends walk right by me on the street? No, ma'am—won't happen."

I packed up my perfect-color cell phone and hightailed it down the aisle. As I rushed past another lipstick display, an azalea-red lipstick with a touch of hibiscus screamed out at me. I pressed on, but I realized I could not ignore the pull of this charming lip color. I turned around excitedly and, holding my phone just so, discovered I had a perfect match. Bingo!

Good heavens—I do sound so very pathetic, don't I? OK, maybe I'll spend a few of my lipstick dollars on a wee bit of lipstick psychotherapy.

Now let me see…what color should I wear to my first therapy session?

UNEMPLOYMENT HITS THE LOVE NEST

Several years ago, during the recession, my Love God joined the ranks of the unemployed. It was a bummer... worse than a week of bad-hair days.

The start-up business did not stay started. You know the drill...bad economy, business sours, customers play hide-and-seek, layoffs start. You see the train coming down the track, but you can't get out of the way because there's nowhere to go. I just braced myself and put away the credit card.

Honey had always worked. He was working when I met him, and—I'm not going to lie—regular employment was right up there on my list of desirable qualities when I was man hunting. So were qualities such as cute, smart, good teeth, funny, and a good kisser. Honey was highly qualified on all counts.

We had always been a dream team of sorts—we earned it, and I spent it. He always had a regular paycheck and took out the garbage every Tuesday night. I was convinced that if I spent all our income, I could help grow the GDP—a public service, really. In fact, the economy started its downslide just about the time my spending fell off. At least that's what Honey always said.

Honey even said his worst fear, now that he was unemployed, was that I had no idea how to "do poor," which was a valid fear, depending on exactly what he meant by "do poor." Did he mean getting a manicure bimonthly rather than monthly? Did he mean one week at the beach instead of two? Or were we talking about cutting my own hair with the hedge clippers? Definitely, maybe I could try to cut back and live on a b-b-b-budget.

To make him feel better, I took the vow of poverty, which was a very focused version of the vow of marriage. It involved complete devotion to coupons, sales flyers, and swearing off new shoes, including the strappy black ones that even the Patron Saint of the Unemployed would have truly loved.

The poverty program got a jump start when we fired the "We Don't Do Windows or Anything Else" cleaning service. Honey declared, "*We* will clean it," and we *did* clean it, for exactly one day, and then *I* cleaned it. But when Honey became unemployed, *he* cleaned it and did a mighty fine job. My gel nails regained their luster once I was not swabbing toilets. With time on my hands, I even organized my closet and made the bed flawlessly. Proof once again that with rain comes rainbows.

Then one Saturday morning, Honey uttered the words of love I'd been dying to hear: "Let's go to the store." Was he was feeling my pain, or were we out of his favorite Fritos Scoops? Who cared? The color was back in my cheeks.

Off to Walmart we went, where we'd do some frugal foraging, as Honey called it. I called them the f-words. He held my hand tightly so that I couldn't sneak away to the clothing aisle to buy...buy exactly *what*? A Vera Wang frock and Jimmy Choo shoes? No, the Walmart clothing is 100 percent acrylic. Not my style—or *not yet* anyway.

"Would you like to go to Quiznos for lunch?" Honey said with a too-wide smile. I didn't see it coming. He was a Trojan horse, a wolf in sheep's clothing. I took the bait.

"Sure...I'd love to!"

"*No! No!* You're supposed to say *no!*" he howled. "It was a test to see if you could do poor, and you failed!" he howled.

"Then don't ask me out for lunch if you don't mean it!" I cried. "You know if it involves food, I'll say yes." I hoped he had built the cost of marriage counseling into the poverty budget.

The poverty thing had not started well, but I was determined to change my habits and to prove to my Love

God that I could do poor. Honey and I are in this together, for better or for worse.

I told Honey how much I loved him, job or no job, because he's my Love God.

COULD IT GET ANY WORSE?

I think I'm a good person. I don't pull the legs off spiders, and I go out of my way not to run over people in the parking lot. I hardly ever steal, except maybe the occasional grape before the bunch has been weighed and paid for at the checkout. A girl can get quite hungry waiting in the checkout line, you know. So given my overall goodness, it's hard to understand why so many bad things happened to me on that awful day.

My troubles began when I was making my favorite three-layer dessert bars for our dinner guests one afternoon. When I poured the second layer on top of the first layer, I noticed that the layers seemed much thinner than usual. Did I forget some ingredients?

Let me double-check that recipe, just to be sure. Yup, yup, yup…got those right. Yup…got a 9 × 9 pan…oh no…I used a 9 × 13 pan! No problem…I'll just whip up a new 9 × 9 pan of thicker bars.

Whew! Problem fixed.

Feeling encouraged by my success, I began the second dessert, which was Canadian butter tarts. I whisked together the eggs and corn syrup and then put that mixture on the shelf in the fridge. *Remember that I did this, OK?*

The recipe then said to pour hot water on the raisins. Raisins? Oh geez—I forgot to buy the raisins! Honey appeared at that exact moment and offered to go to the store. While he was raisin hunting at the Food Kitty, I prepared the brown sugar and butter mixture, which I would add to that egg-and-corn-syrup mixture on the shelf in the fridge, *the one I asked you to remember.*

Honey then arrived home with the raisins, which I dumped into the brown-sugar-and-butter mixture. I filled the pastry shells with this mixture and popped them into the oven until they were baked. As I opened the fridge to put away the butter, I was mortified to see that egg-and-corn-syrup mixture still sitting on the shelf. *Remember that I said this would be important?* I had just baked the butter tarts, having left out half the ingredients and using up the only pastry shells I had!

Honey once again trekked to the store for a dozen more pastry shells. *I know that if I ever have a nightmare involving baking, there will be someone, and I'm not saying who, tossing eggs, raisins, and pastry shells at me.*

Worn out from baking everything twice, I flopped down on the bed to catch up on some *I Love Lucy* reruns while I flossed my teeth with a flossing stick. I had just pulled the floss from between my teeth when I felt a chunk of something in my mouth.

No, it was not a raisin. My tooth had just broken in half.

But with company coming soon, I couldn't worry about a broken tooth because I had to vacuum the gigantic dust bunnies made of yellow Labrador retriever hair. Bless his heart—that dog sheds twice a year for six months each time.

I had just started vacuuming the bathroom floor when suddenly my elbow accidentally knocked my rosy blush powder onto the rug, turning it pink. I continued vacuuming furiously, pushing the beater bar under a rack of clothes in the closet. Out of the corner of my eye, I saw a knee-high nylon disappear into the vacuum, bringing the dust-bunny machine to a screeching halt. *Oh noooo!* The burning smell of the jammed rubber vacuum belt hung in the air. It could not get any worse.

Oh yes, it could.

As I struggled to extract the knee-high nylon from the jaws of the vacuum cleaner, I could hear Honey yelling that he had stepped on the wooden hall floor vent cover and shattered it into many pieces. I realized that if we didn't cover the gaping hole quickly, the wiener dog could slide down the hole just like Alice did. For a split second, I was OK with that—she had has been getting on my nerves lately with her leaks and piddles—but I put my nerves aside and replaced the broken hall vent cover with an unbroken one from the laundry room. The diva dachshund has never done a load of laundry in her life, so there was no danger of her slipping down the laundry room vent.

Despite all these catastrophes, our dinner was fabulous.

But these catastrophes also taught me two useful life lessons: First, it's only a myth that bad things happen in threes—there is no cap on crap. Second, it also taught me that if everything goes smoothly, you have absolutely no stories to tell.

That would be a *really* bad thing.

THE SEA OATEL

It had been a long, hot summer in the city. Honey, our son Braden, Wyatt the yellow Lab, and I were overdue for a visit to the seashore to chill out and kick some sand.

Honey had pored over the online sites of the Outer Banks resorts to find a summer retreat where we could relax, swim, and sit in the sun. Our home away from home needed to accept dogs, which narrowed the list from about 372 four-star resorts to four two-star motels. He finally found one that met our needs. We set out with the "wolf," as my father called him, and all our beach paraphernalia, with barely enough room for my bathing-suit girdle.

We drove down the coastal highway, admiring the glamorous resorts and beach houses with weathered rental signs posted on the balconies. We finally reached our summer home away from home, formally known as the Quality Inn Sea Oatel.

No, that isn't a typo.

Sea oats are a common beach plant and thus the play on words. Cute, huh? But "cute" does not describe my bewilderment at seeing the yellow caution tape wrapped around most of the Sea Oatel property, except for the front desk and pool.

Was I on *Candid Camera*, with Allen Funt about to rise from the dead to say "Smile..."? My Love God explained quickly that we would be across the road in a very nice room where dogs are allowed, and we'd even get a ten-dollar-per-night discount for the sorry state of the Sea Oatel.

We surveyed our new family love nest. Two double beds, too close together. There would be no loving in that nest, for sure. But heck, it was only for four days, and we were here for the sun, sand, and relaxation, right?

Suddenly the Sea Oatel room door flew open, with Braden yelling that Wyatt had jumped in the prickly pear bushes and had green prickles everywhere, including on his paws, butt, and face. We held the woofer tightly, carefully pulling the prickles out one by one. Why couldn't he have fallen into a patch of soft sea oats instead?

Exhausted, we picked up the eight bags of puppy support materials, which included the sun tent, sun umbrella, five towels, water, kibble, leash, lotions, poop bags, and tennis balls and then hustled across the ocean road past the condemned Sea Oatel to the beach.

Wyatt, ignoring his new sun tent, dug a deep hole in the cool, wet sand, out of which his fuzzy head peeked. There he slept while we puppy-sat. No swimming, no beach walks, and no beach balls until the puppy toddler woke.

Prancing down to the ocean, he was the duke of the dunes. Girls in tiny bathing suits flocked to him, oohing and aahing, while Braden and Honey sat riveted, enjoying this female invasion.

I was left to pick the sand out of the Fritos.

Later, as we settled in for the night, I was dismayed to hear my Love God, Love Dog, and Braden snoring in unison. I pulled the pillow over my face, welcoming an early sunrise. I clung to the edge of the love-nest bed to give Honey some man-size space, while Braden and Wyatt slept happily, dreaming of beach bunnies and beach balls, respectively. By morning, after eight hours of immobility, my body had frozen into the shape of a ferret. Only three more nights of vacation bliss left, I grimaced. Could this vacation have been worse?

Yes. The following week there was a hurricane at the beach.

SURVIVING THE GREAT HOLIDAY BAKE-OFF

The holiday season is a friendly and exciting time of year. It's also an incredibly fattening time because cookies, candies, and nuts dance into my mouth when I'm not paying attention. I'd probably even bleed liquid chocolate if I nicked my finger.

Most holiday seasons I beg my Love God to hide all the sweet treats and to dole them out to me if I'm particularly well behaved. But I seem to be a genius at tracking down those treats, just like those snouted animals that root out truffles in France (I just can't bring myself to say "pigs"). It may take a few hours, or even a few days, but if I try hard to think like Honey, I can find them hidden in a cupboard behind the rarely used teacups or on a closet shelf near his rolled coins.

I have even tried hiding goodies from myself, which I know seems odd, but given that my memory isn't what it used to be, it sometimes works. By the time I remember where I hid the chocolates, they have usually grown a white coating, which fortunately scrapes off nicely with a bit of elbow grease.

A few years ago, as the festive grazing season approached, I was worried that I'd once again stuff myself on anything chocolate, leaving no room for high-fiber vegetables from the food pyramid. I'd managed to lose a few pounds just before the holidays, so I really needed a plan to get me through the holiday season looking more like a sprightly elf than a plump Mrs. Claus.

As it was also the season for giving to others, I wanted to bake some cookies to take to my parents when we visited. I gathered the sugar, butter, flour, and melt-in-my-mouth chocolate chips, which I knew I would devour unless I had a good plan for getting through this baking session unscathed.

How could I ever say this to my mom? "Happy Holidays, Mom! I made you some chocolate-chip cookies, but unfortunately, they don't have any chips in them because I ate them all. Hope you enjoy the cookies!"

I first considered wearing oven mitts to make the cookies so that I wouldn't be able to pick up the chips. But this still left me able to pour the chips right from the bag into my mouth, which I confess I've done on occasion without spilling many at all. It was obvious that I needed a much better, elf-proof plan.

Then it came to me…I'd put a large bandage over my mouth while I baked, then no chocolate chips could get past my lips—I could maintain my weight, and the cookies would be chock-full of chips. A brilliant plan!

I applied the bandage carefully, mixed the ingredients, and baked the cookies as fast as I could. Then I stashed them at the back of the freezer, buried among the frozen vegetables where I rarely ventured. I had survived this cookie challenge without one chocolate chip even touching my lips.

Feeling quite proud, I strutted into the bathroom to wash my hands and remove my protective mouth bandage. I glanced up at the mirror to see how silly I probably looked in my bandage but instead was shocked by the bizarre sight staring back at me. There, smudged across the bandage, was an incriminating line of *chocolate dots*. I had tried to stuff those little tasty morsels into my mouth—unconsciously and unsuccessfully—despite having a bandage the size of Rhode Island on my mouth.

At that moment I realized the real power of habit over wishful thinking. Let's face it—it takes twenty-one days to break a habit, not twenty-one minutes. My normal routine was to sneakily eat those little chips, gain weight, and swear to everyone that it must be a thyroid condition because, gosh, I hardly ate a thing over the holidays!

I was doing exactly what I had always done, but this time I got caught red-handed—I mean, chip faced.

THE WEDDING RING

The itchy, red rash started the whole darn business.

I'm referring to the rash on my finger under my rings. It seems that when I removed the rings to cure the rash, I put them in the pocket of my dark-red cranberry purse for safekeeping. I checked the dark corners of that ring-eating thing, where the peanut crumbs and coins mingle harmoniously together. My diamond ring emerged, but my wedding band didn't.

Then came the hard part. I had to confess to my Love God that I lost the ring, and he would certainly remind me that I would lose my head if it weren't attached. I spilled my guts nevertheless. He looked at me with the stare he'd perfected after years of marital bliss.

"You lost the wedding band?" His eyes bulged. "Does that mean we aren't married anymore?" he asked a bit too enthusiastically.

My humility was wearing thin. The best defense is an offense. I struck quickly. "It didn't match my silver jewelry anyway, Honey, so maybe we can replace it with a silver-and-gold two-colored number."

Honey doesn't come from the school of matching jewelry of which I'm head cheerleader.

"It isn't about matching colors," he sputtered. "It is about tradition, our vows, our marriage." His words pierced my heart. All I wanted to do was move on, get a new ring on my finger, and forget about this mess.

Finally, he gave in. "Well, fine then. Let's go look." Score one for the wife.

We went to a mall jewelry store that had lured him with their bright-red half-price signs waving incessantly.

"Do you have anything under fifty dollars?" he asked.

The store clerk looked at him like he'd lost his mind but fortunately chose to ignore him. She quickly brought out trays of sparkly gold, silver, and platinum rings, which were lovely, but far from fifty dollars. However, just to be sure we had found a good deal, Honey insisted that we go to five more stores in two malls to comparison shop.

The promise of a new ring was starting to slip away. Honey declared he'd rather walk on hot coals than consider one more hunk of precious metal. Then, suddenly, I spied the perfect ring. I slipped the white-and-yellow gold circle of love over my quivering digit, just as Cinderella had slipped her foot into her glass Manolo Blahnik.

"This is it! Let's get it," I gushed. It was a bit heavier than the other rings because it was the "comfort fit," and apparently, comfort doesn't come cheap. Before he could ask the price, my comrade-in-rings clerk grabbed it back and headed for the cash register.

Click-buzz-ding.

"Here you go—just put your autograph on this line," she chirped to my Love God.

His face turned white gold, then platinum, and then a pink-gold color. Except for buying the house, cars, and that dark-red rug, I couldn't remember when we'd spent so much money so fast.

As luck would have it, my original wedding band surfaced about three months later in our coin can, where it was hidden among the coins I'd scooped from my purse. Honey suggested returning the comfort ring with the uncomfortable price, but I told him it was stuck on my finger for good.

I think he liked that.

A SOMBRERO IS NOT
A GOLF HAT

The golf tournament invitation arrived in our e-mail like so many other announcements in our new community. I was about to respond with a *no-you-must-be-kidding* e-mail but paused and thought about it. It had been more than twelve years since I'd touched my golf clubs. Even then, I had played golf for only a short time. Never even had lessons, unless you count the instructions that Honey would shout at me when I was swinging wildly at the ball just to get it to go ten feet. Besides playing golf with our kids, I was sometimes required to join my coworkers in an *isn't-this-so-not-fun golf day*, where we played scramble-style golf in which my ball was never the one that went the farthest.

I completely stopped playing when we moved to the Land of Y'all. Too hot, too little time, and too few friends who golfed, so my clubs and golf shoes sat in the attic for more than twelve years until that e-mail invitation arrived. Maybe it's time to start playing again, I thought. Golf was an activity that Honey and I could do together, beyond going to Costco every week or to Phil's Seafood and Propane for jumbo shrimps. I proposed this golf-tournament idea to Honey, and he agreed it would be fun, so I signed us up.

Then reality hit. I had two weeks to learn how to play golf. A trip to the driving range confirmed it was not like riding a bicycle at all. So much to think about. Keep my head down, bend my knees, keep my arm straight—or is it bend my arms, keep my legs straight? Keep my eye on the ball, follow through, lift my heel. Repeat this routine until the ball basket is empty. Go home and nurse sore muscles.

Tournament day arrived, and it was time to get dressed. I recalled the tournament invitation said something about wearing shirts with collars—must apply to the men, I figured. Without a thread of golf wear, I decided on a sleeveless, collarless top. I was almost ready to go but still needed to find some suitable shoes. Sandals are apparently not golf shoes, even if they are coral colored and match my lipstick. My running shoes would have to do. Now where would my visor be? Oh right, I threw it out ten years ago. I found a wide-brimmed woven hat that looked like a sombrero, the kind people buy when their cruise ship stops in Mexico for a couple of hours. It didn't look like golf wear but neither did Honey's baseball cap with a Hurricanes hockey logo.

We were a good match.

Arriving at the golf club early to check things out, I studied the players as they arrived. I noticed that everyone was wearing *real* golf shoes, not sneakers like me. Every single woman had a collared shirt on. Oh geez! I was starting to sweat under my sombrero. Not only could I not golf but also I *looked like* I couldn't golf. I wasn't sure which was worse.

Honey opened the trunk to get the golf bags out, and there in the clear light of day, I saw that my golf bag was covered in thick cobwebs, having been hidden away in the attic for more than a decade. Maybe the cobwebs were a sign that I had no place in this tournament.

It was too late now, so in desperation, I wiped the cobwebs off with my hand to erase all evidence of my golfing hiatus.

Honey and I then joined our partners, a lovely couple originally from New Hampshire. She wore golf shorts, a collared shirt, and golf shoes, just like the e-mail said to wear. She *looked* like a golfer, and a brief introduction revealed she'd been playing for years, as had her husband. This would be the longest afternoon ever—particularly for our partners.

They proved to be very good golfers, for sure, but also patient, kind, and encouraging. Honey gave me tips and reminders, and before long, we'd completed eighteen holes, finishing as a foursome in the middle of the tournament pack.

More importantly, I enjoyed the day so much that I decided I'd become a *real* golfer with a collared shirt, golf shoes, a visor, and a clean golf bag without cobwebs.

Fore!

SHOW-AND-TELL GODDESS

I can tell when it's autumn in Daniel Boone country because my Love God abandons washing the car with his fluffy wool mitt and instead watches hunting and fishing shows beamed into our home from the wild yonder.

As I watch the hunting shows, my thoughts drift back to my childhood. I can clearly remember the deer my father brought home, and the packages of venison wrapped in brown paper which then filled the freezer. It was a mystery meat that Dad tried to pass off as grade A Angus beef. We never seemed to run out of those Bambi bundles, and I was just as happy when our power went out and the thawed, ruined meat had to be destroyed. It isn't the venison, but the dead deer's leg, that I recall nostalgically—the one that was removed just above the knee and then nicely cleaned up. I didn't know what I would ever do with that thing, but when my turn for show-and-tell arrived, I suddenly knew.

Show-and-tell was my favorite activity at school because I had the spotlight to talk about anything I wanted, and nobody would pull me off the stage. Filled with anticipation the night before this event, I usually wandered around the house looking for that special item that would fill my classmates with awe and envy. No picture books or tacky tourist ashtrays of Niagara Falls for this girl. I was going for the big bang, the loud applause, the cheers of lesser gods. So, when I found the deer's leg in the toy box, I knew I had found my ticket to fame.

I didn't connect the leg to a deceased animal with antlers. It was just a dead deer's leg—fur, hoof, ligaments, and all—which we kept in the toy box amid the baseballs, skipping ropes, and roller skates. The leg had a life of its own, and I mean that literally, because when you tugged the ligament just above the knee, the hoof moved. Back and forth, back and forth—I tugged that ligament until the hoof looked like it was waving, much like a queen waving at her subjects. Once Buzzy Munroe saw that magnificent moving leg, I knew he'd choose me to be his girlfriend instead of beautiful Jennifer Eadie with her movie-star name.

In my hoof-waving dreams, I became a show-and-tell goddess, better than even Rosalyn with the wavy blond Marilyn Monroe hair, who could only muster up her leaf collection that she had ironed with wax paper and put in her *Beehive Corn Syrup* scrapbook. Deer's leg versus scrap-book, Diane versus Rosalyn. I would win hoofs down.

When my big moment finally came, I was not disap-pointed. The glory unfolded exactly as I had imagined. I pulled the leg out of the flowered pillowcase for all to gawk at. Oohs and aahs filled the room. I ignored the gri-mace on Rosalyn's face—she knew she'd met her match. The teacher screeched with delight, or maybe horror, and all the boys, including Buzzy, moved in for a closer inspec-tion. This was the recognition I cherished.

As I retired to my seat, dead deer's leg grasped in my hand, I knew I had moved to the show-and-tell Hall of Fame. You could only play the dead deer's leg card once at school, but that was OK—it wasn't that easy lugging around a deer's leg anyway. The leg would retire to the toy box, perhaps for another sister to drag out to secure her popularity.

Though I don't think I will ever get used to the sight of a fallen deer, I am thankful that one such creature gave up its life and leg for show-and-tell history and the fond memories of this one-time child star.

WHAT COLD SORE?

Like many women, I follow a few basic beauty rituals to keep dogs from howling and babies from crying when they see me. These include washing, exfoliating, moisturizing, and even plucking that boingy hairlet on my chinny chin chin. No matter what I do, however, an unsightly blight appears once every few years. I'm talking about a cold sore that starts off tiny and then blows up into a blister the size and shape of Bermuda just under my bottom lip.

So you can imagine my horror when I awoke one Monday morning with a slight itch in the exact spot where my cold sores tend to emerge. It had been more than three years since I had felt the familiar tingle of an imminent cold sore, so I was about due for another eruption. I used to get them about once every ten years, but now it seems I'm on the frequent-flyer program.

A close inspection of my lip in my 10x magnifying mirror showed a little reddish area, slightly raised. Maybe it was just a wee blemish, I fantasized. Or maybe it was the start of a ten-day personal hell when I would have to stay in the shadows so I didn't scare people. It's starting to look like a piece of cauliflower, I think, but reddish.

It could be worse, I reassured myself. I recalled that other horrible rash that broke out all over my face when a dermatologist gave me antibiotics to cure some skin ailment. She warned me that my face would break out in itchy little bumps at first, and I would want to sue her and even call for a revocation of her Hippocratic oath, in which she swore she would do no harm. Ha-ha, I had laughed...how bad could a little old rash get?

Just as the evil doctor promised, it was bad—very bad. I became focused on revenge and reached for the phone to call a skin lawyer. But then I thought, who wants to go to court looking like this and risk having my face plastered on the front page of the local newspaper? Well, maybe not the front page, but I would certainly have made the back of the "Isn't Life Strange" section.

As luck would have it, I was scheduled for a dental appointment the day after the cold sore first appeared. Upon arriving at the dentist's office, I suggested to the receptionist that perhaps I should postpone my teeth cleaning until the cold sore had passed. The receptionist said it would not be a problem and even offered me a prescription to clear up my face flaw quickly, which I eagerly accepted.

The drugstore prepared the prescriptions—I would take two pills every two hours for four days and apply some cream from a micro tube smaller than my baby finger. But the other shoe dropped when I arrived at the cash register. Getting rid of this spot, faster than nature could on its own, would cost $179!

"These medications had better work," I muttered to myself. I swallowed the pills and applied the cream for four consecutive days. The reddish cauliflower blight became bigger, bumpier, and uglier over this period. Perhaps I caught it too late, or maybe the lip gods were punishing me for buying one more tube of lipstick. In any case, I pretended I looked normal as I moved about in public, that I didn't have this big, ugly, red cold sore, and that life was just grand, even though it wasn't.

This cold-sore ordeal continued despite my taking the $179 worth of face-saving drugs. Saturday, Sunday, and Monday passed, and the reddish cauliflower was still there. It wasn't growing. But it wasn't shrinking either. I puffed face powder on it, trying to make it invisible, but instead, it morphed to buff beige cauliflower. Finally, by day nine, the blight had disappeared.

So here's my gripe: cold sores last only ten days *without* the pills and cream! I had reduced my cold sore derma torture by only one crummy day for the money I could have spent at Costco stocking up on cheddar cheese, toilet paper, and laundry detergent.

The next time a cold sore appears, I will just let nature take its course. If I must suffer with a blistering blob on my lip, then at least I won't be poor too.

LISTEN MORE; TALK LESS

The thin young woman sitting across the aisle in the airplane was weeping softly.

She sat slumped in her chair in her pinstripe pantsuit, staring out the window into the early-evening darkness, oblivious to the tears trickling down her cheeks. On her lap, her willowy fingers were anxiously twisting a tissue, as though they wanted to be somewhere else. I stared at her, trying to imagine what painful event had brought on such emotion.

Maybe her grandmother had died in a senior's home after a difficult but happy life. Maybe the young woman had just lost her first banking job and was flying home to her parents for the comfort and solace that only parents can give. Maybe her arrogant boss, who still had his plushy job, had called her into his office, then blurted out the gut-wrenching news—and would she please close the door behind her as she left his office? Maybe she had just stuffed a few personal items in her oversize purse, then arranged with her stunned officemate to mail the box of her books, sneakers, and family pictures to her home.

Or maybe she had just had a lousy interview for a job that she felt would have given purpose and meaning to the past four years in business school. Perhaps the interviewers' questions were robotic, without depth or enthusiasm, as though the candidate ahead of her had clinched the job, and the interviewers were just going through the motions, politely but vacantly. Every interview was crucial these days, as there were so few opportunities.

She wiped the salty moisture from her eyes beneath her oversize glasses, trying hard to stay in control. I sensed that her tears were about a lost job, the story on every family's lips all over the country. Lost jobs, lost homes, lost dreams, lost people.

The young man in the seat beside me chose this moment to engage me in a conversation about his newest degree, showering me with his various business cards and brilliant accomplishments. Even good things happen in a recession to somebody, somewhere, I thought.

I glanced over my shoulder at the weeping young woman, reminding myself that not everyone was having a good day. I wanted to reach out to her, to comfort her, but she seemed so far away across the airplane aisle.

The flight ended, and the passengers did the airplane shuffle, grabbing their oversize bags that had been stuffed into overhead bins to avoid the extra charge, then dragging them down the narrow aisle—thud, bang, clunk. Holiday pleasantries were exchanged with the crew as people hurried to get home to familiar faces. A typical flight in most every way, except for the tears across the aisle.

As I turned the corner toward the baggage claim, I saw the young woman walking slowly down the hallway, pulling her black luggage. The gap between us had closed. I approached her, asking her if she was OK. No, she said, she wasn't. With tears streaming down her face, she told me that her mother had died that morning, but her father had not told her until after her job interview, as he knew this job was very important.

Damn this economy! Why should any job interview be so important that it must come before revealing a mother's death to a daughter? It wasn't her father's fault—it was the tremendous pressure of too few jobs for too many job seekers.

The young woman and I hugged; then we sat down on a nearby bench. I asked her to tell me about her mother— if she had she been ill, what she was like. She talked and talked; we were oblivious to the passing of time. If she were my child, I would want someone to listen, to be there when my child was hurting. Nothing else could possibly be more important at this moment.

How many times in my life had I been so absorbed by my own thoughts that I didn't see the pain or sadness on the faces of other humans? Or I saw such pained faces but ignored them, telling myself that it was none of my business, or that I would be late for something, but most likely nothing.

I vowed at that moment that I will be there for those with burdens greater than mine. I will listen more, talk less, be more observant, and turn away less often.

I won't be so slow to walk across the aisle next time.

PIGS CAN FLY

I'm not Mother Teresa. I haven't saved any souls or changed the world, and I prefer not to wear a head covering due to the hat-head effect. However, I'm proud that I made a commitment to a personal reinvention in 1973, when I was twenty-one, and it all began with just one passing comment from an acquaintance.

One winter afternoon, a fellow psychology student at my lunch table mentioned that she'd just been accepted into an MBA program at another university. Since when did psychology majors get accepted into MBA programs, let alone ever *apply*? This news floored me—you'd think I had just been told that pigs could fly. I didn't know any women pursuing an MBA or even a BA in business. I only knew women in secretarial science—the business program that women were in, back in the day.

I was very traditional in college, graduating in 1973 in psychology like so many other young women who knew more about Betty Crocker than Betty Friedan. That was just the way it was then. I'd tried teacher's college briefly six months earlier, but after teaching the parts and functions of an apple and then tooth decay, I knew I hadn't found my calling.

But because of this single conversation with a classmate, I knew instantly that I too would pursue an MBA. I knew that it was perfect for me. I'd just met a role model. I envied her bold and unconventional career choice, a career option that I'd never even imagined. It was very surprising to me that one casual encounter could have such an influence on me. What if we hadn't sat together that day at lunch?

Everybody experiences moments that have the potential to become turning points in life. One must recognize the opportunity, be bold, be able to dream, and choose to act decisively when the mind or heart is saying it's time to change direction. Don't look back or second-guess yourself, but push forward toward your new goal.

It took me six years after that fateful lunch before I could enroll full time in an MBA program, but I never lost sight of my goal during that time. The day I learned I was accepted, I handed in my resignation at my social-services job. In 1981, I finished my MBA and joined Xerox, where, six years later, I met my Love God.

See, pigs really can fly.

ACKNOWLEDGEMENTS

This book would never have been completed without my husband's encouragement, confidence in me, and patience. He gives me strength when I falter. He makes everything more fun. He can laugh when called Honey or Love God by our neighbors. He is the yin to my yang and the Desi to my Lucy. I love you so much, Eric!

Thank you to our children, my sisters and my wonderful friends who read my stories and laughed with me over the years. Your encouragement has meant everything to me.

Meredith Durkee, my niece, created a cover illustration that was better than I could ever have imagined. It still makes me laugh! Thank you so much, Meredith, for the beautiful cover and all your support with my book.

It takes a village to produce a book, I have learned. Thank you to Pam Roth for all her support and guidance, and to Eliot Sefrin who gave me great advice on my stories, as well as on my unique punctuation and use of the English language.

And many thanks to Christine Davis for her broccoli-salad recipe.

ABOUT THE AUTHOR

Diane Pascoe has a BA in psychology and an MBA. She worked in human resources for many years while writing her candid and hilarious reflections on everyday life for this funny memoir. In addition to winning prizes in writing contests, Diane's humorous essays are regularly featured in local publications.

She lives in North Carolina with her husband, Eric (also known in these stories as "Honey" and "Love God"), and their two dogs. Four grown children in their blended family are scattered throughout the United States and Canada.

When Diane isn't writing, she's managing her lipstick addiction—for which, thankfully, there is no cure.

63354757R00093

Made in the USA
Middletown, DE
01 February 2018